japan

the informal contained

● ● ● ellipsis

japan

the informal contained

First published 2000 by
●●●ellipsis
2 Rufus Street
London
N1 6PE
EMAIL ...@ellipsis.co.uk

ISBN 1-899858-46-6

Publisher Tom Neville
Designed by Jonathan Moberly
Layout and image processing by Heike Löwenstein
Drawings by John Hewitt
Glossary by Andrew Wyllie
Index by Diana LeCore
Printed and bound in Hong Kong

British Library Cataloguing in Publication Data: a catalogue
record for this publication is available from the British Library

contents

Mythology maintains that the Japanese islands were borne of the deities Izanagi and Izanami, as were the islands' sister and brother, the Sun goddess Amaterasu and the Storm god Susanowo. The conflict of Susanowo caused the retreat of Amaterasu to a cave and, thus, darkness engulfed the world. Amaterasu was enticed to return by the other inhabitants of the 'Plain of High Heaven' and was rewarded with the expulsion of Susanowo. He and his henchmen descended to Izumo on the south-west coast of Honshu, the main island of the archipelago, and fathered Japan's earliest inhabitants. Amaterasu, established at Ise on the south-east coast, sent her grandson Niniji armed with a sacred mirror reflecting her image and with a host of retainers to receive their submission. The first emperor, identified as Niniji's great-grandson, Jimmu Tenno, is reputed to have founded his capital in the vale of Yamato, the site of later Kyoto, in

1 **Matsue, reconstruction of a pit-dwelling.**

From the outset the Japanese sought to live in harmony with nature: even in primitive pit-dwellings of c. 5000 BC the portico extended before the entrance breaks the barrier between internal and external space.

660 BC. His clan, the people of Yamato, descend from his great-grandfather's retainers.

Geology suggests that the Japanese islands were produced by volcanic activity along one of the main fault lines in the earth's crust, where the Pacific and Asian continental plates clash. Constantly subjected to earthquakes, the islands stretch from the subtropical to the subarctic zones, and the clash of cold and warm fronts over them produces heavy rainfall in the spring and the autumn, typhoons in the hot summer, and frigid winters. Sensitively attuned by necessity to these unstable seismic and climatic conditions, and thus empirical by nature, the original Japanese found their origin in the clash between sun and storm, naturally worshipping the forces of nature.

The archipelago arcs into the Pacific opposite Siberia, Manchuria and Korea, and its inhabitants are diverse in origin. The indigenees (called Ainu) apart, some may have derived from the Malay islands to the south, but the majority seems to have come from Mongolia through Manchuria and Korea. The most significant among these at the dawn of Japanese history are the Yayoi. Probably crossing in waves from the Korean peninsula during the 3rd century BC, they imported both rice cultivation and the facility to work metal – at first bronze, then iron. Metal-working ensured their triumph over the natives and earlier immigrants, and it was clearly related in the mythology: Amaterasu's mirror, traditionally reproduced in bronze as the key object of ritual devotion by the Yayoi, reflected her devastating countenance, of course, and the invincibility of metal.

Though generally assimilated into one hybrid race, the immigrants had been organised into clans ruled by chiefs from time immemorial. Each clan had a patron deity, the personified fertility spirit (*kami*) of its district identified with a prominent hill, waterfall or tree. All were also devoted to the fertility spirits of the deceased – especially deceased leaders – and to those of the Plain of High Heaven – above all to the arch-protectress, Amaterasu. The imperial family emerged with the clan that first asserted significant hegemony over its neighbours from Yamato. Ise was in its orbit and Ise's celestial inhabitant, Amaterasu, was identified as their ancestral deity. Under her, their supremacy was acknowledged by most of the clans of Honshu and the other main islands of the archipelago, Shikoku and Kyushu, in the so-called

Kofun period (c. 300–700 AD), but their political authority was never absolute.

Since the triumph of Yamato shortly before its inception, Japanese history has been moulded by an idiosyncratic conservatism: change was admitted – or forced – but existing institutions were supplemented, not supplanted. The key to this is the divinity of the emperor: descended from heaven, unlike the Chinese emperor who only held the mandate of heaven (*qi*) as long as he was effective, any development had to be accommodated to his indispensability.

Early buildings

Remains unearthed by archaeologists – clay models and images inscribed on sacred objects – indicate that the first Japanese buildings were shelters over pit-dwellings,[1] followed somewhat later by granaries raised from the ground on piles. The earliest remains of the former type, doubtless indigenous, date from the mid-proto-neolithic period known as Jomon (after the cord pattern applied to its pottery) of c. 5000 BC. More sophisticated versions, usually accompanied by the raised granaries of wet-rice farmers, are common at sites associated with the Yayoi.[2]

2 **Yayoi settlement with pit-dwellings and raised store-houses** clay model (Himeji Historical Museum).

Pit-dwellings were of variable shape, size and depth. Though usually rough squares c. 4 by 4 metres (13 by 13 feet), later they were also curved and nearly twice as large, but rarely were they ever deeper than 1 metre (3 feet 3 inches). A pitched, hipped or hip-and-gabled roof of reeds or thatch laid over timber rafters was carried on four or more posts connected by tie-beams. These defined the central living area from the lateral ancillary spaces covered by eaves descending almost to ground level. Central stone hearths appear in the 5th millennium BC. Notwithstanding the inundation of their land for wet-rice farming, the Yayoi seem to have sustained the tradition, with shallower pits, raised wooden floors and embankments. The pitched roofs of the later, larger examples generally had a ridge pole raised on king-posts to the front and rear.

The granaries, perhaps also the houses of the rulers, were usually raised on four, six or eight piles. The platform was wooden and occasionally extended beyond the line of the posts to form a gallery. Sometimes there were wooden walls of horizontal or vertical slabs attached to the posts on both ground and upper levels, but usually the ground was not enclosed. The posts were braced by tie-beams and the lateral ones might be connected by rafters to form a loft. Hip-and-gabled roofs were still common, but the open gables of the simple pitched form reveal a ridge pole supported by additional posts, free-standing to front and rear. An image of a raised building on an engraved mirror from Samida Takarazuka (early 5th century AD) suggests that the ends of the rafters extended beyond the apex to either side. This was probably to secure the thatch and was later done with billets laid horizontally across the ridge at regular intervals between rafters crossed diagonally at the ends.

Yoshinogari, one of the largest Yayoi settlements so far uncovered, has circular and rectangular pit-dwellings, raised store-houses, wells and watch-towers, and tombs.

The pit-dwelling tradition was sustained for a millennium at least – increasingly sporadically. The raised store-house was never supplanted. Indeed, it was adapted for the aristocratic dwelling and was sanctified as the prototypical shrine, beyond which it was always an essential element in the sacred enclosure.

Burial practices

The Yayoi were buried in urns or trenches, sometimes covered by low mounds. The earliest rulers of Yamato, the first emperors, were buried in hills – if not demonstrating disparate origin, certainly asserting superiority. Their successors were further dignified with man-made tumuli: indeed the period of Yamato supremacy is called Kofun after the 'old mounds' with which the Japanese first achieved monumentality. Not necessarily indebted to the Indian stupa (see volume 5, INDIA AND SOUTH-EAST ASIA, pages 36–37) – the hemispherical burial mound is ubiquitous – but probably inspired by the tombs of the imperial Han in China, the Japanese tumulus was uniquely extended with a trapezoidal element for obsequies on a base with the profile of a keyhole and set into a D-shaped moat.[3]

200 m

600 ft

The spirit house

With agriculture came continental influence on the concept of the shrine – indeed, on the conception of the deity. Over several centuries following their introduction of rice cultivation, the Yayoi developed rites to encourage crop fertility that provided the basis for the native animistic pantheism – which was nameless until the mid-6th century when the Bud-

3 Bakai, Osaka Prefecture, tomb of the 15th emperor Nintoku early 5th century AD, plan.

Natural hills sometimes provided a basis for tombs, but for man-made mounds the extraction of earth readily formed a ditch that could be flooded to form a moat. Like the tomb of Nintoku (430 metres long by 40 metres high/1400 by 130 feet), and the even larger one of his successor, the most ambitious exercises have three moats, but some have none at all.

The imperial tombs are inviolate, but the form was not exclusively imperial: excavation of aristocratic Kofun has revealed that trenches for wooden coffins were gradually replaced by increasingly substantial stone chambers for stone sarcophagi as masonry technology was introduced to Japan from Korea in the 5th century.

4 Embellishment on the back of a ritual mirror from Nara Prefecture bronze, early 5th century AD (Imperial Household Department).

Of the four shrine buildings represented, one has a thatched roof rising directly from the ground, like a pit-dwelling; another has a similar roof rising over a podium; and a third reproduces the same form of roof – presumably

dhists distinguished it as Shinto, 'the Way of the Gods'. Dedicated to the propitiation of the fertility spirit and involving bronze regalia, the Yayoi seem to have focussed on granaries hardly distinguishable from the grandest of human dwellings, but doubtless erected in an enclosure protecting the objects sacred to the spirit concerned.

Timeless was the belief that the spirits of the dead were disembodied ghosts who would haunt their former homes indefinitely unless provided with a special 'spirit house'. However, it may not have been until the Kofun period that the Japanese first began to see the fertility spirit in human form and, therefore, as in need of dwellings – or at least of somewhere to keep their sacred regalia. The anthropomorphic deity was acquired by Indian Buddhists from Hellenised western

hip-and-gable – over a trabeated pavilion raised on piles and surrounded by a verandah with a ladder. The fourth shrine building, also with piles, verandah and ladder, has a gable roof. The roof ridges project beyond the base plane of the gables, producing a deep overhang, and the raked rafters are extended to cross on the diagonal at the apex, as a finial (chigi).

Asia and was transmitted to China in the early centuries of the Christian era. Though Buddhism was probably introduced to Japan in the mid-6th century, the anthropomorphic representation of deities may well have preceded it.

Despite its identification with the tomb, the greatest legacy of the Kofun period is the archetypical spirit house of the native religion. Images on the backs of ritual mirrors of the 5th century provide the essential link with the Yayoi granary – or aristocratic residence.[4] Raised on stilts, rather than dug from the ground, entered from the side and covered by a steeply sloping thatched roof supported by free-standing posts and penetrated by extensions to the raked rafters at each end, the spirit houses anticipate the most sacred of all Japanese shrines, those accommodating the Sun goddess Amaterasu and the Rice god Toyouke bime no okami, with their treasures, at Ise. Attributed to the 3rd and 5th centuries respectively, the spirit houses are supposed to have been rebuilt every 20 years from their inception, but building is first recorded at Ise in 685. Thus, though the buildings are new, the form (Shinmei zukuri) is of venerable antiquity.[5–8]

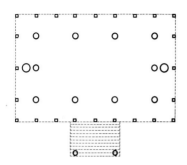

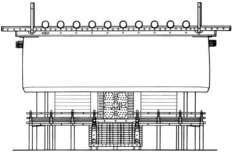

5 **Ise, Shinto shrine, Shinmei style.**

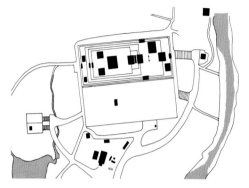

6 **Ise, inner sanctuary, shrine, Naiku** 5th-century site
with building first recorded in 685, and rebuilt for the 61st
time in 1993, plan.

There are two separate sacred compounds at Ise: the
inner sanctuary, known as Naiku and dedicated to the living
presence of Amaterasu (late 3rd century), and the outer one,
known as Geku, dedicated to Toyouke and built to match
the earlier work c. 200 years later. Each sanctuary has two
adjacent sites used alternatively for the rebuilding every 20
years prescribed by imperial decree at the outset. The main

A conservative tradition

Nothing demonstrates more graphically the conservatism of the Japanese tradition than its record of continuous reproduction. The native trabeated system was expanded in accordance with Chinese models for temple and palace, and further developed for diversification of space. There were even moments when decoration was as opulent as anything produced in China; and tile often replaced thatch for greater security, but the superbly worked timber of Ise characterises Japanese building throughout its history.

While much of this is due to the belief – common throughout the world – that it is impious to tamper

shrine, centred within its sacred enclosure and accompanied by symmetrically disposed store-houses, preserves the regalia of the deity – most notably the mirror given by Amaterasu to her grandson Niniji and transmitted by him to the imperial line through his great-grandson, the first emperor, Jimmu Tenno. Each is associated informally with a higher shrine for the god's living presence and a lower one for the local fertility spirits. The hierarchy between these secondary shrines is taken to represent the subjection of the indigenes of Ise by the imperial clan from Yamato.

7 Ise, outer sanctuary, shrine, Geku view from the outer precinct to the entrance of Naiku, the inner sanctum.

Within four palisades, the main shrine building in Naiku (shoden, 11 by 5.5 metres/36 by 18 feet) is raised on posts set into the ground without a base – like the traditional granary. The central post (shinno mihahira) perpetuates the sacred pillar, facilitating the descent of the deity, which seems to have been the focus of the earliest Japanese sanctuaries. Surrounded by a verandah protected by deep eaves, the enclosed chamber is entered through a door from a staircase in the centre of the southern side. The thick thatch of the pitched roof is held down by 10 billets evenly spaced along the ridge between the crossed rafters that frame the gables like barge boards. Subsidiary store-houses in the compounds and extraneous shrines dedicated to the fertility spirits related to the dedicatees are similar in conception. The Ise style of building draws its effect from splendid timber and superb carpentry, unmasked by paint.

Each site, and each sanctuary, is entered through a succession of portals (torii), initially establishing the bounds of sacred ground. Consisting simply of two cylindrical posts surmounted by an overhanging lintel and braced towards the top with a secondary beam, the portals are an invariable feature of all Shinto sites.

8 Ise, inner sanctuary, Naiku.

The shrine is dedicated to the living presence of
Amaterasu. Note the immaculate carpentry, the superb
unpainted cypress (hinoki) wood, the deep overhang of the
ridge pole supported on a freestanding post, and the
diminishing thickness of the thatch. The original function of
the stout pegs that punctuate the end rafters is obscure.

with forms adopted by the gods – though originated by priests – much is also due to the role of the carpenter. His was certainly not the world's only hereditary craft with conventions transmitted orally (at least until the publication of manuals in the 17th century), but more than most others – except the Chinese – Japanese building followed sanctified formulae rather than the drawings of individualistic architects, and the standardisation of the trabeated form in whole and part meant prefabrication in the carpenter's workshop. Moreover, the carpenter went into the forest to choose the timber required, registering the characteristics derived from the aspect of each tree to ensure for it the same aspect when it stood dressed in the re-evoked forest of structure. And sensitivity to nature is – or was – the prime characteristic of Japanese building.

Local variations

There are other Shinto sites almost as venerable as Ise, and distinctive styles of shrine developed in them in sympathy with the local vernacular. Sumiyoshi, Osaka, was dedicated by the empress Jingo (late 4th century) to the gods of the sea under whose protection her dynasty was established: three gods each have a shrine, facing the sea in line; she has the fourth, set apart from the others. The shrines were low buildings, of four bays by two with pitched roofs and entered through the gabled end rather than the side, unlike the Ise type (see 5, page 19) – and contrary to Chinese practice. Sumiyoshi is the main source of inspiration to Shinto builders in western Japan. Izumo, in Shimane Prefecture, is the centre of the cult of Amaterasu's grandson Niniji whose grand shrine (taisha) was not only more elevated than those of Sumiyoshi, and square with two bays to each side, but also it had a pitched roof and a bifurcated entrance under a gable. It was emulated elsewhere in the area – at Matsue, for example, where the existing Kamosu shrine predates the present version of its model.[9,10] Throughout Shimane the Taisha style is represented at countless sacred spots, though on a tiny scale.

Variously related in style to these most venerable structures are the many later shrines built for the guardian deities of new capitals and new regimes: for instance, Kyoto's Kamo shrines, dedicated to the Heian deities when the capital was moved from Nara at the end of the 8th century; the Hachiman shrines of the war-spirit who guarded both Nara and Kyoto;[11-13]

9 **Matsue, Kamosu, shrine** origin remote and obscure.

The shrine conforms to the Taisha style of building established at Izumo, but the present building predates the rebuilt prototype of 1583 by 161 years. The stairs to the pile-supported chamber are covered by a separate roof in the centre of the gabled entrance front, but the entrance is dislocated to one side by the symbolic central post between the twin bays; the passage to the inner sanctum is also deflected by another central post supporting a screen only to the right. The crossed finials perch on the gables detached from the rafters or barge boards with which they originated, and are decorative features characteristic of the Taisha style and related styles developed later elsewhere.

10 **Matsue, Kamosu, shrine** detail of the central pillar deflecting the entrance, and the crossed finials.

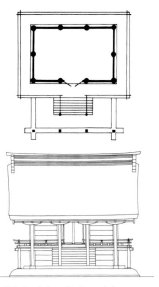

11 Kamo, Shinto shrine, Nagare style.

This style is entered through the long side like the Ise style (see 5, page 19), but the roof is projected asymmetrically out over a portico in an unbroken curve.

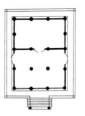

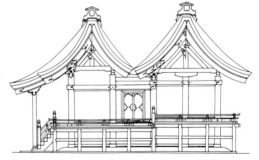

12 Iwashimizu, Kyoto, Shinto shrine, Hachiman style.

This style has two contiguous halls of the Nagare type (see 11, page 29) under roofs of their own, the front one extended to form a portico.

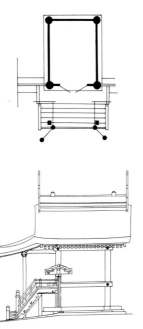

13 **Nara, Shinto shrine, Kasuga style.**

14 **Nara, Kasuga sanctuary** shrine to the fertility spirit of the site, the Wakakusa hill *yami*, traditional construction first recorded in the 12th century.

The shrine repeats the form of the four main Fujiwara shrines. As in both the Sumiyoshi and Taisha styles, the pile-supported chambers are entered up a roofed stairway through the gable end. The four corner posts are braced just above ground level by sills. Like Taisha shrines, the Kasuga ones have crossed finials perched on the gables, and like the Sumiyoshi ones the timber structural frame is vermilion and the timber walls are white. As elsewhere there are detached shrines for fertility spirits related to the main deities.

15 **Nara, Kasuga sanctuary** 8th century, last rebuilt in 1863, verandah before the four shrines in the main compound.

As at Sumiyoshi, the main sanctuary encloses multiple identical shrines: here four small structures (1.8 by 2.6 metres/6 by 8 feet) are aligned side-by-side to accommodate the tutelary deities of the Fujiwara. A 9th-century description makes it clear that there was a barrier before the four shrines, but it was replaced by a verandah in the 12th century, itself subject to periodic rebuilding.

or the Kasuga shrines of the Fujiwara clan on the slopes of Wakakusa hill at Nara, established in the 730s and elevated to quasi-imperial significance when the Fujiwara assumed the regency. The Kasuga style at Nara has much in common with the Sumiyoshi shrine, and even has features related to the Taisha, but the shrines in the main Fujiwara clan complex, screened by detached verandahs, seem to derive from a portable prototype like the palanquins provided for the deity at many Shinto sanctuaries.[14,15] In all these types, except the Hachiman, there are crossed rafters at the apex of the roof, though usually detached from the structure as purely decorative elements – as at the Kamosu shrine at Matsue (see 9–10, pages 27–28).

At the height of the Kofun period, early in the 6th century, the emperors had sent expeditions to Korea and even established a colony there. Through this involvement with the mainland, influence flowed from China – especially through script. Confucianism readily inspired the education of the imperial élite and lent its authoritarian shape to their conception of the state. It informed Japan's primitive pantheism, too, given that both were concerned with the propitiation of ancestral spirits and were preoccupied with the proper performance of rites rather than with theological speculation. Any unfulfilled inclination towards the latter, however, was satisfied by Buddhism, which had begun to filter through to Japan by the mid-6th century, embracing animism there – as at its inception in India – and complementing Confucianism – as in China. Indeed it was the Buddhists of the Mahayana (the Great Vehicle, or the Broad Way) who coined the term Shinto (the Way of the Gods) for the native animistic pantheism, and the Japanese have usually followed both.

Japan's first Buddhist temples

The first Buddhist temple was founded at the command of the emperor Kinmei (539–71) to house an image of Sakyamuni (the prince Siddhartha of the Sakya, whose domain was on the border of modern India and Nepal, and who was the historical Buddha) sent to him by the king of Korea in 552. The foundation was followed by an outbreak of the plague which discredited the faith and provoked the destruction of the temple. However, the new faith was not without powerful supporters, particularly the head of the formidable Soga clan, who maintained that the worsening of the plague testified to the anger of the Buddha. Strife ensued but Soga overcame the anti-Buddhist, anti-foreign forces in 588, founded a new capital at Asukadera (south of Nara) and installed his niece as empress Suiko (593–628), pending the accession of the late emperor's son Shotoku Taishi. This never happened, but the prince acted as regent from 593 until his death in 621. Codifier of law, regulator of government, cementer of relations with China and Korea, patron of Buddhism, he is revered for his compassion, scholarship and love of the arts.

With the aid of monks and craftsmen from the Korean kingdom of Paekche, the empress Suiko built a new Buddhist temple, Hokoji, at Asukadera in 596. The regent is credited with the foundation of Shitennoji (in the south of Osaka) in 592, in gratitude for Soga's victory of 588, and with the inception of Horyuji (beside one of his palaces north-west of Asukadera) in 607. Others followed. Nothing remains of earliest Hokoji. There was a disastrous fire at Horyuji c. 670, followed by highly important rebuilding; but much of Shitennoji was perpetuated in faithful renovation until the Second World War and has subsequently been rebuilt in its original form.[16] That reflects early Chinese Buddhist practice in the axial alignment of the principal elements: gatehouse, pagoda and image pavilion. It also marks the introduction of Chinese building types and construction techniques.

Distribution and form

The sacred enclosure is ubiquitous, but instead of the Shinto portal the Japanese Buddhist compound, like the Chinese, is usually entered through a succession of small columned halls with side chambers or niches for the images of guardian spirits (*nio*). The outermost gate is normally to the south, the inner main precinct gate is usually centred in the main compound's cloistered enclosure. Outside, to the north, twin pavilions house the belfry and library. Also out-

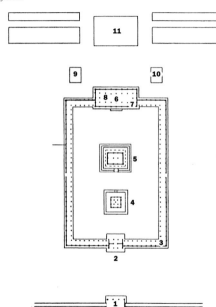

side were the dormitories, refectory, storerooms and other utilitarian structures.

To dominate compound and countryside in enshrining relics or sacred texts, the Japanese Buddhists developed their version of the Chinese pagoda, itself translated from the Indian stupa in terms derived from the Han multi-storey, trabeated tower (see volume 8, CHINA, page 30). Invariably of timber and square in plan, unlike the earliest surviving Chinese examples which are polygonal and of masonry, the Japanese form (*to*) has an odd number of storeys each distinguished by deep eaves: five, as at Shitennoji, is the usual number.[17]

To house their images, and later, to accommodate congregations for lectures (in the main image hall and the lecture hall respectively), Japanese Buddhists

16 **Osaka, Shitennoji** late 6th century, rebuilt mid-20th century, plan.

(1) South gate (nandaimon); (2) main precinct gate (chumon) in (3) cloistered gallery (kairo); (4) pagoda; (5) main image hall (kondo); (6) lecture hall (kodo) with (7) aisle (hisashi) and (8) nave (moya); (9) belfry (shuro); (10) library (kyozo); (11) dormitory (sobo).

retained the Chinese type of oblong trabeated hall.
Entered through the central bay of one of its longer
sides, this usually has a nave flanked by an aisle on at
least one side, and covered by a wide-eaved hipped or
hip-and-gabled roof. For greater dignity, the nave
rises well above the aisle over a clerestory and it carries a distinct roof, as in the rebuilt main image hall
of Shitennoji.

17 **Osaka, Shitennoji** view along the principal axis of the
compound from the entrance.

Note the podia, the trabeation and the wide-eaved hip-
and-gable hall roofs. In contrast with the axial alignment of
gate, pagoda and main image hall, excavations at Hokoji
have revealed the foundations of twin pavilions (presumably
for images) either side of the pagoda as well as a larger one
on the main axis. In both complexes there seems to have
been an additional hall for assembly and lecturing at the
head of the axis, outside the compound at Hokoji, centred
on the north cloister range at Shitennoji. The arrangement
at Shitennoji conforms to early Chinese practice as
represented by the Dacien si (Temple of Great Goodwill) at
Xi'an (see volume 8, CHINA, page 90). Hokoji seems to
follow a Korean precedent – Chungam Ri near Pyongyang.

For dignity and for protection from the damp, as on the mainland, halls and pagodas are usually set on separate podia of impacted earth sheathed in stone and punctuated with stone bases for the timber posts (as in the rebuilt Shitennoji). Their centres defining the bays, the posts are braced with longitudinal and lateral beams. Walls to the rear, sides and sometimes the end bays of the front are non-load-bearing: if not of timber slabs, they may be of wattle and daub or of mud and straw. The lateral beams, called 'rainbow' (koryo) because of the slight upward curve which enhances their tensile strength, usually bear only king-posts carrying the ridge of a pitched roof over buildings one bay deep, but in larger, taller structures they are repeated on a smaller scale at a higher plane over struts. With the widening of bays, even the longitudinal beams carry intermediate supports for the superstructure, often in the shape of an inverted V, called 'frog-leg' struts (kaerumata), as on the lower storeys of the rebuilt Shitennoji pagoda and main image hall. These appear in the earliest images of the trabeated structure at Yungang (see volume 8, CHINA, pages 81 and 83).

As in China, too, increasingly sophisticated bracket clusters, carried first on the posts, later also on the

beams, allowed for the lengthening of intercolumniations and the deepening of eaves (as at the outset at
Shitennoji). Also, the outer bracket arms and upper
beam ends hold the purlins, or diagonal beams which
themselves then hold the purlins, on which the rafters
are laid. Doubled for important buildings, sometimes
radiating at the corners, the rafters carry the tiles that
– after the example of China – generally distinguish
Japanese Buddhist temples from the thatched or shin-
gle-roofed Shinto shrines.

Experiments in plan

In the 7th and early 8th centuries there was considerable experiment with varying the distribution of the
main elements in the temple complex. Bi-axial symmetry was developed with twin main image halls
aligned on a cross-axis running through the pagoda or
twin pagodas aligned to either side of a main image
hall, or symmetry was abandoned with the siting of
one pagoda and one main image hall side by side. The
cruciform arrangement of main image halls was
adopted for the Hokoji temple, for instance. The twin
pagoda approach, conceding predominance to the
central main image hall, distinguished the Yakushiji

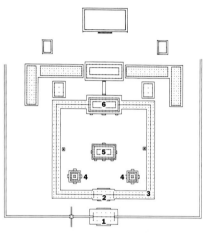

18 **Nara (vicinity), Yakushiji** founded 680, plan.
(1) South gate; (2) main precinct gate; (3) cloistered gallery;
(4) pagodas; (5) main image hall; (6) lecture hall.
    Founded to house an image of the bodhisattva of
Healing (Yakushi Nyorai in Japan), the complex has been
entirely rebuilt at various times (including the 1990s) with
the probable exception of the original eastern pagoda
(35 metres/114 feet high).

19 **Nara (vicinity) Yakushiji** view across the compound to
the eastern pagoda (right), with a rebuilt pagoda and main
image hall (left).

The eastern pagoda is unique for the alternating rhythm
of three full storeys with prominently projecting eaves and
three mezzanines (mokoshi) with moderately projecting
eaves. If not actually dated to 680, the pagoda is usually
placed within the following century.

monastery complex near Nara,[18] but only one of the original pagodas survives.[19] Predating the latter, asymmetry is splendidly represented by the Horyuji where the main image hall and pagoda are side-by-side, rather than on axis with the main precinct gate.[20]

The construction of these buildings after the fire that destroyed prince Shotoku's complex in 670 was reputedly completed by 714 and as there is no record of their subsequent rebuilding, they seem to be the oldest-surviving timber structures of importance in Japan – perhaps, indeed, the oldest surviving timber buildings in the world.[21-23] A later lecture hall, beyond the main compound to the north, was replaced in the 10th century and the compound was extended to include it.[24-25] In the mid-8th century a secondary sanctuary

20 **Nara (vicinity), Horyuji** after 670, main compound (sai-in), plan.

(1) Main precinct gate; (2) cloistered entrance; (3) main image hall; (4) pagoda; (5) library; (6) belfry; (7) lecture hall. The dormitories and refectory are to the east of the main compound.

On falling ill, the emperor Yomei (540–87) was persuaded by his son, prince Shotoku, to embrace Buddhism

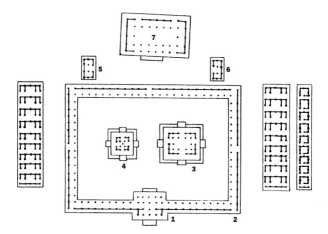

and to dedicate a temple to Yakushi Nyorai. The emperor died within months of his conversion, but the prince fulfilled the vow and built the temple beside a small palace to its east. Contemporary chronicles record its dedication and destruction by fire in years corresponding to 607 and 670 respectively: excavations at the site have revealed an axial distribution comparable with that of Shitennoji (see 16–17, pages 38 and 40). The new asymmetrical temple, built slightly to the north-east and perhaps incorporating as lecture hall a Shotoku shrine saved from the fire, was substantially complete by 710 when the imperial capital was established at Nara. The secondary sanctuary, on the site of prince Shotoku's palace compound, was developed from 739. Soon after, the conversion of a palace building from Kyoto into a lecture hall to the north of the octagonal shrine (hakkakudo) seems to have set an important precedent.

It is now generally thought that the main compound as built after 670 was a simple quadrangle with the north and south cloisters equidistant from the main image hall and pagoda. The belfry and library would then have been outside the compound to the north. Further north a hall, added probably towards the mid-9th century, was burnt in 925 and replaced in 990 with a palace building from Kyoto adapted to form a lecture hall. The cloister was then extended to embrace belfry, library and lecture hall. All the elements of the complex were listed in an official document of 731, except for the lecture hall. At that time a dormitory seems to have occupied the site of the present lecture hall, but an inventory of 747 lists a refectory (larger than the present one) after the main image hall: it is possible that this was the original building at the head of the north–south axis and that it doubled as a lecture hall.

21 **Nara (vicinity), Horyuji, main precinct gate** late 7th century.

Slightly to the west of centre in the southern range of the cloistered enclosure, the unusual twin passages through the two-storeyed gatehouse are flanked by Japan's oldest guardian statues, dating from 711.

22 OVERLEAF **Nara (vicinity), Horyuji, main compound** with main image hall and pagoda aligned on the east–west axis. The pagoda's three storeys are carried on a grid of four columns and a colossal central mast.

23 **Nara (vicinity), Horyuji, Denpodo** section.

Set on a stone base, the aisle and nave have distinct roofs with broad eaves, the latter rising for greater dignity over the unused space of a blind attic surrounded by a balustrade carried on brackets and intermediate frog-leg struts. An outer aisle, added in the late 8th century, has its own contracted eaves. Over the main columns, strengthened with pronounced entasis, simple bracket arms bear the beams. At the edges the arms are extended to hold a diagonal beam that, counterbalanced by the main roof, carries the outer purlins of the over-sailing eaves. The sculpted props at the corners of the upper storey were added in the early 18th century.

On the central dais, under the canopy of a coved ceiling, Shakyamuni (the historical Buddha of 623, reputedly modelled on prince Shotoku) is flanked by Yakushi Nyorai (607) and Amida (the Buddha of the Western Paradise, early 8th century) and accompanied by the guardians of the quarters of creation (early 8th century). They were surrounded by celebrated murals, destroyed by fire in 1949. Colour is confined to a dark red wood stain in contrast with plain white-washed walls, but as main image halls were called golden halls there was presumably much gilded detail, inside at least.

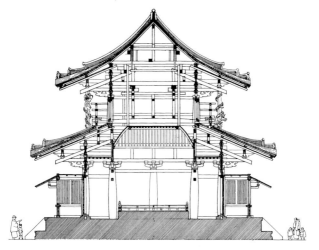

5 m
15 ft

24 **Nara (vicinity), Horyuji, Denpodo with library (background).**

25 **Nara (vicinity), Horyuji, Denpodo** interior.
Flanked by the bodhisattvas, Yakushi Nyorai (left) is the main one.

26 Nara (vicinity), Horyuji, Yumedono in the eastern sanctuary 8th century, view from the south-east with the northern assembly hall (background).

Built on the site of the prince's palace to house his statue, the octagonal shrine is the earliest of several similar ones in the Nara region.

Between the two compounds are the refectory, stores and dormitory. The southern end of the latter was converted into a shrine to Shotoku (Shoryo-in) in the 12th century.

27 **Palace pavilion** detail of a 15th-century scroll painting of the life of prince Shotoku (Kyoto National Museum).

This type of rectangular hypostyle hall, initially undivided internally, though partitionable with screens, is known as a shinden (sleeping hall). Instead of the podium, which elevated the earliest Chinese-style temple halls, the posts rise from the ground and there are also balustraded verandahs – as in earlier Yayoi shrines and granaries (see 2, page 11).

was developed on the site of prince Shotoku's palace around an octagonal shrine[26] and a palace hall, of the open-plan type known in the secular context as shinden (denpodo), was donated by the emperor.[27]

After the death of prince Shotoku in 621, then of empress Suiko in 628, the Soga manipulated the imperial succession and seemed bent on usurping the throne for themselves. In 645 their overweening head was assassinated by two imperial princes in league with Kamatari Fujiwara of the Nakatomis, rivals of the Soga. The puppet empress abdicated and one of the princes acceded to the throne as Kotoku, initiating the Taika era of reform under the guidance of Kamatari. A stream of edicts recast Japan on the Chinese model, furthering the regulation of government on the humane lines laid down by Shotoku but bolstering imperial power after the eminent Tang example – unenduringly, as it transpired.

The impact of Buddhism was magnified: along with statecraft came priests and architects and a new capital, Naniwa, emulating Chang'an (see volume 8, CHINA, page 41).[28] An imperial edict of 646 instituted Buddhist cremation rites and prohibited burial in Kofun. Another edict of 685 ordered all householders to erect altars to the Buddha. The simplicity of the Shinto shrine paled before the magnificence of the temples that proliferated throughout the imperial domain, yet there was no concerted effort to popularise the reli-

heijokyo (nara)

28 Naniwa (modern Osaka) model of palace, mid-7th century (Osaka Castle Municipal Museum).

Excavations on the site of the seats of the emperors Kotoku and Temmu (d. 686) provided the basis for the reconstruction of an imperial palace on the Tang model.

A port from time immemorial, Naniwa was unplanned, unlike its successors, as imperial capital. There seems to have been a palace there before Kotoku moved his capital from Asuka in 645, and his palace, completed in 651, was superseded by another a century later. The huge compound (4 by 3 kilometres/2.4 by 1.8 miles), equivalent to the Imperial Forbidden City in Beijing (see volume 8, CHINA, page 181), was initially divided onto two zones, the southern one (Chodoin) for administration and the northern Inner Palace (Dairi) for the imperial family. Entered from

provided ample space for development along the
grand formal lines of Chang'an adapted to the traditional local pattern of rice-paddy division in squares.
Though far from complete, the new city, Heijokyo,
was formally occupied in 710.[29]

Religion and state

A district east of the site was set aside to accommodate
Buddhist temples moved from the old capital, distort-
ing the axial plan. Of the four main ones two were
moved from Asukadera, the Yakushiji was moved
from Fujiwara and the Fujiwara clan temple of
Yamashinadera was rebuilt as Kofukuji in association
with the Kasuga shrine of the clan fertility spirits. And
new ones were to be built by Buddhist priests and
architects imported from China.

Following Tang precedent, the emperor Shomu
issued an edict in 741 establishing a network of provincial monasteries and convents dependent on two great
national temples to be built in Heijokyo: the monastic
Todaiji, which had the exclusive right to ordain priests,
and the conventual Hokkeji. Amaterasu, the Sun
goddess, had provided the emperor with his native
mandate: he now sought another from the Buddha in

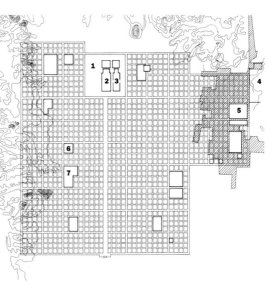

29 **Heijokyo (modern Nara)** plan.

(1) Imperial compound (Daidari) with (2) Chodoin (court for administration) and (3) Dairi (private apartments); (4) Todaiji; (5) Kofukuji; (6) Toshodaiji; (7) Yakushiji.

Settled in prehistoric times, Nara was an early centre of the rulers of Yamato, but it does not appear to have taken primacy until the empress Genmei moved there. The new city (4.8 by 4.3 kilometres/3 by 2.5 miles) was divided into regular blocks by 10 streets running east–west, eight running north–south, and a central axial thoroughfare (72 metres/236 feet wide) leading from the main southern gate to the state entrance of the palace compound in the north. Like its predecessors and successors, the latter had four distinct zones: an outer court dominated by an assembly hall (Choshuden); the court of the ministers surrounded by 12 pavilions for the different branches of administration (Chodoin); the court of ceremonial audience dominated by the principal imperial hall of state (Daigokuden); and the inner compound of the imperial private apartments (Dairi). This last was initially to the east of the Daigokuden in a precinct of its own. After 750, the Daigokuden, Chodoin and Choshuden were relocated on axis with the Dairi, to its south in an extended compound. The original buildings in the western compound were adapted for use by the empress consort, but the Choshuden was moved to the Toshodaiji (see 39, page 82). Even after the departure of the court in 794, Nara remained an important regional and, above all, religious centre.

his drive to weld disparate clans, each devoted to its own fertility spirit, into a centralised state – and neither he nor his Tang mentor was the first emperor to see the essentially universal appeal of the Buddhist salvation ideal as an instrument of unity.

Until this time Buddhist theologians in Japan were primarily Hinayana (the Small Vehicle) in their affiliations, especially in their obsession with canon law, but now they turned to the Mahayana (see volume 5, INDIA AND SOUTH-EAST ASIA, pages 53–80). Reserving release from the brutal cycle of existence to the monk who was able to give up all worldly concerns in the pursuit of enlightenment, the Hinayana was essentially the way of an élite. The implications of a state religion were, of course, very different: offering salvation to the masses in virtue of faith in the ministrations of a supremely compassionate deity, in contradiction of the exclusive claims of the monk in virtue of personal responsibility exercised through mental and spiritual discipline, the Mahayana was bound to prevail so long as the humanitarian ideal of prince Shotoku and the Taika era guided imperial reform. In fact, it was predominant well before the end of the Nara period.

Given the essentially compassionate ideal of the historical Buddha, Sakyamuni, the Mahayana postulated that there must have been other Buddhas for the other aeons of creation. The corollary of the universality and infinite multiplicity of Buddhahood is the bodhisattva: if everyone has the essence of Buddhahood, enlightenment, and as the goal of enlightenment is salvation from the cyclical course through the evils of this world, then myriad supremely compassionate spirits who have attained Buddhahood (bodhisattvas) will have renounced its end in their concern to guide the suffering to their own salvation. In Japan, veneration of Sakyamuni (Shaka in Japanese) was supplemented with, ultimately supplanted by, devotion to various manifestations of the Buddha, in particular to Bhaisajya (the Buddha of Medicine – Yakushi in Japanese), Amitabha (the Buddha of Boundless Light – Amida in Japanese) with his attendant bodhisattva Avalokitesvara (the Lord of Infinite Compassion – female Guanyin in Chinese, male Kwannon in Japanese). And in Japan the protective bodhisattva was readily identifiable with the native fertility spirit.

Led by the priests Genbo and Roben, who had studied in China, the Kegon sect of imperial theologians built their state religion on Buddhist holy writs (*sutras*) devoted to the centrality and protection of Buddhahood, most notably the so-called Lotus Sutra (Hokkekyo in Japanese, drawn from the Sanskrit original), its Sino-Korean permutation (Avatamsaka Sutra, Kegongyo in Japanese) and the Sutra of the Benevolent Kings (Ninno-kyo in Japanese). The basic postulation – of obvious relevance to an imperial regime – is that Buddhahood is an absolute, central to myriad universes, and that it unfolds through all creation like the petals of a lotus: that the Buddhahood of Sakyamuni, far from the achievement of the individual, is identical with the essential nature of all being and responds to ministration like the flower to the sun.

The establishment of the state religion was marked by the creation of a colossal statue of the Universal Buddha (Vairocana, Roshana in Japanese) as the chief icon of the principal state temple, Todaiji. Conceived by the emperor Shomu in 740, after he had seen an image of Roshana in a provincial temple, the imperial deity was seated on the 1000 petals of the lotus, which traditionally symbolised the unfolding creation of the universe in all its multiplicity (and had its obvious analogy in the emperor and the unity of his diverse realm). Precedents were set by the Tang and their predecessors at Yungang and Longmen (see volume 8, CHINA, pages 78–79), but there the images were cut from the living rock. Shomu's Roshana was cast in bronze from a mould 16 metres (52 feet) high. And the main image hall required for its shelter at Todaiji was larger even than the largest halls of the Tang palace at Chang'an.

Before casting was complete, enough gold was found to gild Shomu's colossus. Amaterasu was consulted. She consented. The Buddha was assimilated to the sun and with this act of high state the essentially popular process of assimilating Buddhism and Shintoism had the grandest possible inauguration.

The imperial temples

The imperial temples of Heijokyo followed the imperial Chinese axial norm, unlike Horyuji (see 20, page 47), but varied it in multiplying the principal elements. Thus the scheme of Todaiji provided a large, central main image hall in a vast compound flanked by twin pagodas to the south-east and south-west, with a lecture hall and service buildings to the north, and the ordination pavilion to the west.[30–31] At Kofukuji, two

30 Heijokyo (modern Nara), Todaiji plan.
(1) Pagodas; (2) Daibutsuden (Great Buddha Hall);
(3) lecture hall; (4) refectory.

Founded by the emperor Shomu in 743 for the Kegon sect (introduced into Japan from China in 735 by the priest Roben), Todaiji was dedicated in 752. Preceded by two monumental gates (of which the Nandaimon was the greatest) the Daibutsuden was unprecedented in scale for a timber building (57 by 47 metres/187 by 154 feet and 52 metres/171 feet high). Entirely surrounded by a verandah and two aisles, the outer one under its own, lower, roof, it was joined by colonnaded galleries to subsidiary pavilions, as in images of Tang palaces. To the north, the lecture hall had a precinct of its own framed to the north, east and west by dormitories.

The Kaidanin (ordination hall) was beyond the main compound, to its west. West-north-west is the Shosoin, a store-house built of dressed logs for treasures given by the emperor and others: it is one of two notable survivors from the original foundation (though restored in 1913). Apart from the Tegaimon (a much-renovated gate) and store-house, the other survivor is the Hokkedo (Hall for Meditating on the Lotus Sutra) in a precinct to the east.

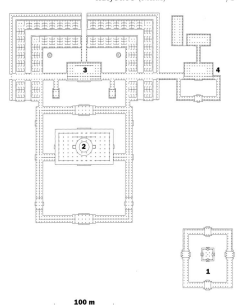

100 m
300 ft

31 **Heijokyo (modern Nara), Todaiji** model of the original foundation, mid-8th century.

32 **Heijokyo (modern Nara), Todaiji, Hokkedo or Sangatsudo** c. 746, lateral section.

Reputedly the main image hall of the priest Roben's original Konshoji of the Kegon sect, the classic simplicity of its form and structure (five by eight bays, with single-step brackets, squared rafters and a ceilingless, hipped roof) is wholly consistent with such a date. Whereas the images in the Horyuji main image hall were arranged to address all directions (see 23, page 53), denying frontality, all except one

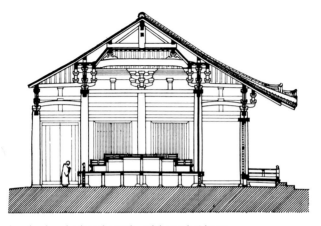

here faced resolutely to the south, and the north aisle was screened off as a sort of sacristy. The structure is lucid too: simple vertical struts provide intermediate support between columns, and bracketing (two tiers inside, one outside) responds purely to functional requirements. Adapted to accommodate the rites performed annually in celebration of the Lotus Sutra, it was extended to provide more space for the participants and witnesses in the late 12th century (see 64, page 139).

supplementary lecture halls were to be interposed between the main one and the twin pagodas. Only one of the pagodas was built, but the Todaiji project was fully realised on a site four times larger than the Kofukuji. Both Kofukuji and Todaiji were burnt in 1180, though the latter's subsidiary Hokkedo survived.[32]

A full picture of the mature Heijokyo temple is provided by the Toshodaiji founded in 759. The main image hall, enshrining a superb contemporary image of Roshana flanked by Kwannon and Yakushi Nyorai, is original except for the roof raised in the 17th century.[33] Built by Chinese immigrants, it is the greatest extant example of Tang architecture, except for the Eastern Great Hall of the Foguang si (Temple of the Buddha's Glory) at Wutai Shan (see volume 8, CHINA, page 103), which it must greatly have resembled before its roof was changed. Like its larger lost contemporaries, Kofukuji and Todaiji, it is a monumental rectangular hypostyle hall with a symmetrical cross-section, though the arrangement of screens provides an open verandah for worshippers along the front.[34-37]

33 **Heijokyo (modern Nara), Toshodaiji, main image hall** interior.

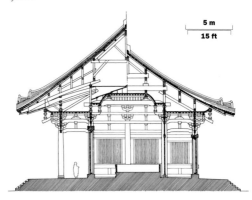

34 **Heijokyo (modern Nara), Toshodaiji, main image hall** mid-8th century with a 17th-century roof (the original roof is reconstructed on the right), lateral section.

The main image hall of seven by four bays (28 by 14.6 metres/92 by 48 feet) is unusual for its period (in Japan, if not in China) in having only one storey. The distinction of the front range of bays as an open verandah before the other three ranges enclosed as the nave was novel and it set an important precedent (though symmetry in the section is

35 Heijokyo (modern Nara), Toshodaiji, main image hall from the south.

disturbed only by the screening of the north aisle, as in the Todaiji Hokkedo) (see 32, page 73). The intercolumniations are graded in width from the sides to the maximum in the centre. Stepping forth in their serried ranks, triple brackets support rectangular rafters and a diagonal lever arm which, in turn, supports a fourth bracket holding a circular purlin.

36 **Heijokyo (modern Nara), Toshodaiji, main image hall** verandah.

37 **Heijokyo (modern Nara), Toshodaiji, main image hall** detail of eaves.

38 **Heijokyo (modern Nara), Toshodaiji, dormitories and store-houses** 8th century.

To the east, beside the dormitories, the treasure and *sutra* stores (hozo and kyozo respectively), raised on piles and walled with logs dressed to a triangular profile and chamfered at the corners, are among the earliest surviving examples of the adaptation of the ancient indigenous granary type.[38] The lecture hall, on the main axis to the north, was imported to the site from the imperial palace in 760.[39-40] With a verandah, like the main image hall, it anticipated the development of the lecture pavilion as a hall with icons enshrined in the main space and the devotees accommodated in one or more extra aisles open to the front, which was furthered in the 9th century by newly introduced esoteric sects.

Palaces

Nothing survives on the Heijokyo palace site, indeed no secular building of the period survives unaltered. Though both adapted to changed circumstances and were much renovated, however, the imperial palace halls reused for the lecture hall of the Toshodaiji (see 39, page 82) and the Horyuji Denpodo (see 24, page 54) well demonstrate that the Chinese hypostyle prototype, enclosed with shutters or non-load-bearing wall

39 Heijokyo (modern Nara), Toshodaiji, lecture hall
from the south-west.

Moved from the Choshuden compound of the Nara
palace in 760 (see 29, page 64), the lecture hall was renovated
in the 13th century, but it retains much of the original
structural system, notably double rainbow beams. In
distinction from the main image hall, and that type's norm,
it has a hip-and-gable roof.

40 **Heijokyo (modern Nara), Toshodaiji, lecture hall**
interior.

panels and subdivided internally only by movable screens, was as important to palace builders as it was to the Buddhists. Before the construction of Nara, that example was well established at Naniwa (see 28, pages 60–61) where the formidable alignment of courts and halls on a north–south axis clearly emulates Chang'an. The Chinese masonry podium survives at Toshodaiji (see 39, page 82), but it cedes to the indigenous trabeated platform surrounded by verandahs in the Horyuji Denpodo, as in numerous later re-evocations on scrolls (see 27, page 57).

The Heijokyo temples founded by imperial decree were originally conceived as sanctuaries for the protector of the realm. However, with grants of virgin lands and tax exemption to the monasteries that developed around them, the power of the priests became a threat to the imperial authorities at Nara. It was to escape from this, indeed, that the emperor Kammu moved the capital to Heiankyo (Kyoto) in 794. The plan was an amplification of Heijokyo's grid, and temple construction within the new imperial city was limited to two main sites – the Toji and Saiji, by the south-eastern and south-western gates respectively. In fact, the western half of the project was never realised and the Saiji site lapsed.

The introduction of esoteric sects

About the time the emperor moved to the new capital, several novel esoteric sects were introduced to counter the power of the Heijokyo establishment. Favoured by the emperor and his advisors, the most important were the Tendai and Shingon. In general, they preferred remote sites for their unorthodox rites, the Tendai establishing its headquarters on Mount Hiei, overlooking (ultimately overawing) Heiankyo, the Shingon on Mount Koya way off to the south-west. Significantly, however, the Shingon were given the Toji site within Heiankyo and perhaps the Saiji site would have gone to the Tendai, had it been developed.

In the later Nara period various schools of the Mahayana were introduced to Japan from India via China, and they promoted much metaphysical debate: to the Madhyamika (Sanron in Japanese) contention that all in the material is illusory, the Yogacharya (Hosso in Japanese) responded that all in the universe is a construct of the mind. In reply the Avatamsakas (Kegon) of Todaiji – the principal recipients of imperial patronage – interpreted the universality of Roshana in terms of consciousness, and saw all sentient beings as facets of the universal mind. The new sects discounted mind.

The Tendai scholars maintained that the Buddha was the ultimate reality beyond both matter and mind, apprehensible neither to empiricism (as they agreed that the phenomenal world is illusory) nor to transcendental idealism (as individual consciousness is equally illusory) but only through the instruction of the *sutra*s – revelation. Like the Kegon sect, they took their departure from the Lotus Sutra, identifying the historical Buddha with the essence of the universe in absolute terms, and at the popular level they furthered the identification of the host of bodhisattvas with the native pantheon – the fertility spirits of Mount Hiei above all. There the emperor sanctioned the ordination of priests in the Tendai temple – named Enryakuji after Kammu's era – independent of the Nara hierarchy who had hitherto guarded the rite exclusively.

If the Tendai was the most metaphysical of Japanese sects, the Shingon was occult. Its proponents distinguished between the exoteric and the esoteric, the revealed and the secret, the body and spirit of Roshana, the world and the mystery of life. To penetrate that mystery, to gain access to the realm beyond consciousness, like the Tibetan Lamaists and the devotees of Tantrism in general, they sought to invoke occult powers through the chanting of magic formulae. And they too won popular support by identifying fertility spirits as emanations of Roshana, especially at Koya.

The path to feudalism

Eclipsed at the centre of power though they may have been, the old Heijokyo clerical hierarchy's tax privileges were sacrosanct, but the emperor Kammu had some success against the secular magnates who posed a similar threat to his authority and financial security. He abolished the hereditary tenure of civil office, particularly provincial governorships that disposed of large tax-free estates as quasi-independent rulers. His success was limited and his successors found it difficult to sustain. He and his successor also pursued a war with the Ainu – the native tribes who had never been assimilated – in which advance was largely due to Sakanoue Tamuramaro who was rewarded with the title of Sei-i-tai Shogun (Barbarian-subduing Great General).

Peace and prosperity encouraged later 8th-century emperors to lapse into learning and to leave the concerns of government to their chief advisor, the Fujiwara *Kampaku*. With the advent of the *Kampaku* the unity of the imperial ideal became duality: the emperor was supplemented, not supplanted, by a hereditary Fujiwara regent (*sessho*). The Japanese looked for continuity in the emperor's descent from the original emperor Jimmu Tenno, who brought them under unified control. His legitimacy as their ruler was assured by their common descent from the Sun goddess Amaterasu – rather than from some inferior foreign invader – and, in the event, the longevity of his line amassed its own prestige. As the fount of legitimate authority the emperor could not be destroyed by one of his officers without the destruction of that officer's claim to power. No one, not even the most grandiloquent Fujiwara, dared take that step. Nor did the Fujiwara overawe the emperor with military might, as others were to do later: they dominated through marriage into the imperial line.

Successive young emperors were married to Fujiwara daughters and persuaded to abdicate in favour of their first son: obviously the Fujiwara's position as regent for his grandson, the child-emperor, was bolstered by the status of his daughter, the empress-mother. Beyond that, the other progeny of the now quasi-imperial Fujiwara formed a court aristocracy that provided the major officers of state. Even as provincial governors, however, they remained at court, and power was administered by the local clan chiefs (*daimyo*) who were quick to take advantage of the situation. With the grant of landholding in reward for imperial service and the concession of the right of private ownership over newly reclaimed land in the mid-8th century, the centralised state succumbed to feudalism.

The apogee of the Heian period was achieved by the Fujiwara in the first half of the 11th century. By then, however, the problem of ensuring that there was always a daughter to marry the emperor – let alone a son of the union – had led to the emergence of several co-lateral branches of the Fujiwara, and abdicated emperors began to assert themselves. The failure of a Fujiwara bride to produce an heir led to the accession of the forceful emperor Go-sanjo (1068–72), and for more than a century from the 1070s the emperors Shirakawa and Toba in turn held more effective power than the *Kampaku* even after retiring to monasteries.

Meanwhile, abbots were allowed to raise forces from their tenantry ostensibly to protect themselves from the incursions of the Ainu. Enryakuji, in particular, had a formidable force that was in practice often to overawe the government in Kyoto. Not to be outdone, the local clan chiefs also maintained armies. Rival factions at court appealed to rival chiefs, whose professional warriors (*samurai*) made them the real powers in the land.

With the isolation of the court from reality at Heiankyo by the 10th century, devotional emphasis in the imperial entourage shifted to personal salvation.

Following the trend at Chang'an in the decline of the Tang, inspired by devotion to Guanyin, priests such as Eshin (942–1017) wrote with beatific vision of rebirth in the Land of Purity for those with faith in divine mercy. This anticipated overwhelming devotion to the long-venerated Amida and Kwannon, through whose grace the faithful soul would be reborn in the Pure Land of the Western Paradise (Sukhavati, Jodo in Japanese).

Developments in temple building

Sympathetic to nature, the esoteric sects rejected the formal norm of temple planning developed on the relatively flat sites around the old capitals. Moreover, while the old sects initiated the practice of building subsidiary sanctuaries on detached sites that did not compromise the order of the main one – such as the Yumedono of Horyuji or the Hokkedo of Todaiji (see 26 and 32, pages 56 and 73) – the free situation of the new sects promoted the proliferation of image halls dedicated to different aspects of the deity within a single, irregular compound – such as Koya of the Shingon or, failing the survival of the original Toji, their Daigoji on the outskirts of Kyoto, and Enryakuji of the Tendai

on Mount Hiei. To serve their particular purposes, too, the new sects both maintained and transformed old building types.[41]

After the introduction of the Mahayana to Japan, devotees presumably gathered in the space in front of the main image hall, resorting to the lecture hall for instruction. With their emphasis on abstruse ritual, the new esoteric sects tended to combine the two halls into one building for worship integrated with assembly – or at any rate to eclipse the former with the latter. To

41 **Kyoto, Daigoji, pagoda** mid-10th century.

The temple was founded in 907 under the patronage of the emperor Daigo (897–930) for Shingon monks entrusted with prayers for the emperor and the nation (hence it is known as Daigo Shingon). The initial building in the original upper precinct (Kami Daigo) was the Yakushido (Hall for Yakushi), followed by the Shakado (Hall for Sakyamuni) in the secondary lower precinct (Shimo Daigo) in 926 and a five-storey pagoda between 936 and 951. The former was destroyed, like almost everything else in the complex, in the civil wars of the 15th century and was replaced in the 16th century; but the latter survives, reputedly as Kyoto's oldest building.

provide more places in the refectories and dormitories of expanding monasteries, the hypostyle hall was readily extendible – with the roof ridge longitudinally, or doubled laterally under parallel pitched roofs. The provision of extra space for worshippers in image halls was more complicated, especially as the logic of the type of hypostyle hall imported from China required matching adjuncts to front and rear (and sides, indeed), though the images enshrined in the centre were worshipped only from the front.

The progressive solution was to retract the altar platform to the back of the nave, leaving the north aisle free for ritual circumambulation (pradakshina), and to add yet another range of extra bays to form an antechamber under an extended or separate roof to the front. The earliest examples are known only from texts or are deduced from excavation, but the procedure was anticipated in the Tendai Enryakuji Komponchudo and Monjuro.[42-44] A more elementary approach, anticipated in the main image hall at Toshodaiji, was to double the aisle between the nave and the entrance (with a magobisashi if covered by an extension of the aisle roof; a mikoshi if under its own pitched roof), or to build a detached range in front of

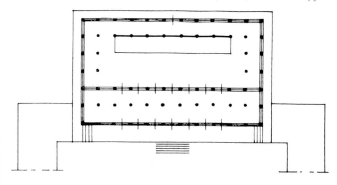

42 **Mount Hiei, Enryakuji, Komponchudo** 9–10th centuries, plan.

43 PREVIOUS PAGES **Mount Hiei, Enryakuji, Komponchudo** main court front.

Mount Hiei, abode of the fertility spirits of Kyoto, was the retreat of the monk Saicho (767–822, later known as Dengyo Daishi) in 785. The initial building of the complex, which became one of Japan's most powerful monasteries, was Saicho's meditation hall (dedicated to Yakushi on its consecration in 788). Saicho introduced his esoteric Tendai doctrine in 805, after a pilgrimage to China, and built a shrine to Manjusri, bodhisattva of Wisdom (Monju in Japanese) on the hill above his original meditation hall. He also requested imperial sanction for the ordination of his sect's priests on Mount Hiei beyond the auspices of the Heijokyo establishment at Todaiji: this was granted and an ordination hall (kaidan) was completed 5 years later. Towards the mid-9th century the founder's hall was rebuilt on a colossal scale as the Komponchudo (Root Hall): facing the unusual cloistered court, its outer aisle appears to have been doubled soon after, and again during renovations in 978. It was destroyed with the rest of the monastery by Oda Nobunaga in 1571, but is believed to have been reproduced in reconstruction from 1624.

Enryakuji has three main sanctuaries: Toto, the earliest with the Komponchudo as its nucleus, Saito and Yokawa.

44 **Mount Hiei, Enryakuji, Monjuro** shrine on the upper level, interior.

A miniature two-storey pagoda-like structure, this building was also destroyed by Oda Nobunaga and reproduced in the 1620s. Though on a minute scale, the interior well represents an antechamber for worshippers screened from the image chamber.

the building. The Nagare and Hachiman types of Shinto shrines reflect the development of the magobisashi and mikoshi respectively (see 11–13, pages 29–31), and the detached range is represented by the relatively late verandah screening the four shrines of the Fujiwara Kasuga sanctuary (see 15, page 33). Doubled aisles were doubtless common in shrines of all esoteric sects. Early examples accommodating worshippers of Kwannon and Amida at Hokaiji and Koryuji show the transition from a simple verandah.[45–47] A more developed example is the antechamber of the main image hall at Ishiyamadera.[48]

Of course, the effect of developing an antechamber was an asymmetrical section and end profile – a magobisashi could usually be contained without disturbing symmetry, as at Koryuji and Hokaiji, but larger survivors are wanting. Ceilings, at first over the main space, later over the extension as well to mask any disparity, allow pitch to be increased to span both elements with one roof for greater visual effect outside without exaggerated vertical perspective inside. In construction and detailing, roof and ceiling were often quite disparate in an elaborately framed system called 'hidden roof' (noyane) (see 46–47, pages 103 and 105).

45 **Kyoto, Hokaiji, Amidado** 1057.

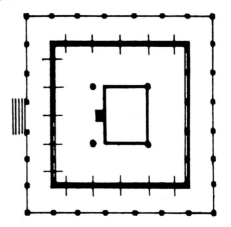

46 Kyoto, Hokaiji, Amidado plan and section (right).

The square hall, of five by five bays, is surrounded by a
verandah one bay in depth, has a nave of a single square
bay, wider than the outer ones, and a residual ambulatory
considerably wider than the verandah. Syncopated, the
outer and inner structures could not be braced in the
traditional perpendicular system of lateral and longitudinal

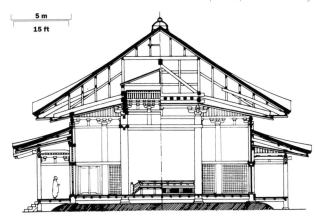

5 m
15 ft

beams: instead, there is an *ad hoc* arrangement of slanting beams on semi-diagonal lines hidden between the ceiling and the roof. Coved and coffered, supported on bold but single-tier brackets, the ceiling recalls the Toshodaiji main image hall (see 34, page 76). Prophetically, the central bays of the verandah are given special emphasis by the raising of the line of the eaves over chamfered posts.

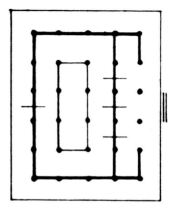

47 Kyoto, Koryuji, lecture hall 1165, plan and lateral section (right).

The temple was founded in 622 in honour of Shotoku, but it was transformed in the 12th century when the worship of Amida was becoming predominant in court circles. The lecture hall, enshrining Kwannon, is its oldest remaining structure. Four bays deep and five long, it is partitioned so that the first range of bays forms a semi-enclosed vestibule (one bay deep) instead of a verandah, as at Hokaiji (see 46, pages 102–103). Like the rear range of bays

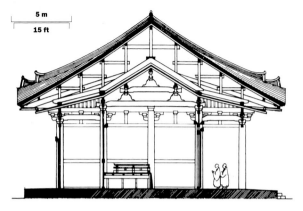

that forms an aisle behind the image platform of the nave, the vestibule has a low-pitched ceiling distinguished from the higher structure in the centre. The roof was probably raised over a hidden structure at the outset, with continuity of line at a steeper pitch than either of the ceilings to mask their disparity, to enhance monumentality and to throw off the rain. The columns are tall and slender, lacking entasis, the beams lose their subtle curvature and the frog-leg struts have double-curved profiles: late Heian architecture tended towards lightness and grace from strength and virility.

48 **Ishiyamadera, main image hall** antechamber.
The temple was founded c. 750 at the base of the sacred
Mount Garan, seat of important fertility spirits, by the

The western paradise

The climax of Heian temple building took place under the later Fujiwara and was emulated by the resurgent emperors after 1072. The Hojoji of Fujiwara no Michinaga, begun c. 1019 on the Kamo river to the north-east of Heiankyo, and the Hosshoji,[49] dedicated in 1077 by the emperor Shirakawa on the stream named after him, both had halls linked by colonnaded galleries to the north, east and west of a lake. The huge, central main image halls, on stone platforms, were dedicated to Roshana, but there was an almost equally grand hall for Amida to the west of

Kegon priest Roben at the instigation of the emperor Shomu as one of the chain of provincial temples dependent on Todaiji. The oldest surviving structure, from the late 11th century, is the nave of the main image hall and its adjunct, a shrine to the lady Murasaki Shikibu (975–1031), who wrote the celebrated romance *Genji Monogatari* (*The Tale of Genji*) there in the early 11th century. The veneration of Kwannon was important at the site, as at other temples of the Nara period, and it is likely that extra space was needed for worshippers in the main image hall. The extant outer structure dates largely from the late 16th century.

49 **Kyoto, Hosshoji** 1077, plan.

(1) Amidado (Hall for the Worship of Amida); (2) nine-storeyed pagoda; (3) main image hall; (4) bell tower and *sutra* store; (5) lecture hall; (6) Yakushido (Hall for the Worship of Yakushi); (7) Godaido (Hall for the Worship of the Five Wrathful Gods); (8) gates.

Though the main image hall was dedicated to Roshana and the western hall houses Amida, the whole scheme evokes the native land of the historical Buddha Sakyamuni in the conventional Tang terms of a palace with many halls, the central one with rectangular galleries leading to pavilions by a lake. The nine-storey pagoda on the island to the east of the Amidado, to the south of the main image hall, perhaps recalls a passage in the Lotus Sutra relating the miraculous appearance of a huge stupa out of the earth before the Buddha. Added to the temple by 1083, 5 years after the dedication of the main halls, it was burnt in 1342.

50 OVERLEAF **Uji, Byodo-in, Hoo-do** 1053.

Developing an earlier villa for his retirement, Fujiwara Yorimichi built the Hoo-do as a shrine to Amida and a reception hall. It is a small shinden with limited internal division, in the Heian tradition, joined by lower wings to pavilions overlooking the lake.

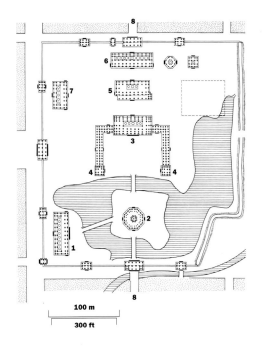

100 m

300 ft

the lake in both schemes. The garden setting ameliorated formality, as it did later in palace design: indeed, as emperors retired to the duties of monastic rule and lived in the context of the temple, there was no clear distinction between religious and secular modes at the apex of society.

Hojoji and Hosshoji are long vanished, but something of their splendid symbolism survives, miraculously. An Amida hall was occasionally built as an adjunct to a palace in the age of the late Fujiwara, like the exquisite Byodo-in added by Fujiwara Michinaga's son, Yorimichi, to his villa at Uji, south-east of Kyoto, in 1053. In the art of Tang China, the Pure Land was generally represented as the Palace of the Western Paradise, in allusion to the royal origin of the Buddha, and the model was inevitably the emperor's palace at Chang'an (see volume 8, CHINA, page 43). Conforming exactly to the type most commonly represented in the Tang frescos of the Buddhist grottoes at Dunhuang, for example (see volume 8, CHINA, page 75), the Hoo-do (Phoenix Hall) of the Byodo-in is the most tangible surviving record of the Tang ideal in secular architecture.[50]

Heiankyo: city and palace

Like Heijokyo, Heiankyo conformed to the grid imported from China – like the later imperial city over which modern Kyoto is built. By decree, as at Heijokyo, the houses of Heiankyo also followed the Chinese courtyard model – the number of courtyards doubtless reflecting social standing in the majority. The aristocratic house seems to have consisted of a main shinden, subdivided by screens and surrounded by verandahs as before (see 27, page 57), but linked to smaller pavilions by galleries like the Hoo-do of the Byodo-in at Uji, though not necessarily symmetrically (see 50, pages 110–111). The galleries would also have defined garden courts but as they were open, they allowed for the visual integration of these external rooms.[51]

As to the palaces of the Heian rulers – emperors and regents – little remains. However, excavation, contemporary descriptions and paintings confirm the conformity to Tang models conveyed by the close relationship between the Hoo-do and the images of the Palace of the Western Paradise in the caves at Dunhuang (see volume 8, CHINA, page 75), which accord with the excavated remains and images of the palaces of Chang'an. Like these, and prefiguring

51 **Palace pavilions** detail from a 15th-century scroll painting of the life of prince Shotoku (Kyoto National Museum) (see 27, page 57).

The shinden, at the bottom, remains predominant, but now it is linked by bridges or galleries to smaller pavilions devolved into the garden at right angles to one another.

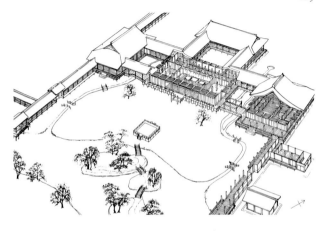

52 Reconstruction of a Kyoto lake-side palace late
Heian Fujiwara era.

The central shinden (shown unroofed to reveal the
internal screening) is linked to side pavilions by galleries
bordering the lake.

Hojoji, the Kyoto palace of the Fujiwara regent Tamemitsu (942–92) had a central hypostyle hall, south-facing over a lake and entered in the centre of the south front, joined by galleries to subsidiary pavilions north, east and west, and further galleries extending south from the eastern and western pavilions to frame the lake.[52] Of the same type as the Horyuji Denpodo (see 24, page 54), the central shinden provided the main living space, in which tatami matting probably made its first appearance as a regular floor covering. Elsewhere excavation suggests that the disposition of a lake to the south dictated entry from east or west and, in turn, that the lateral alignment of elements encouraged the native predilection for asymmetry.

Though rebuilt most recently in 1855, the Imperial Palace (Gosho) in Kyoto represents the development of the so-called shinden style of building in the later Heian period.[53–58] By then the emperor – and his most affluent subjects – were no longer satisfied with an open-plan hall. Movable screens – or curtains – were replaced with sliding ones to define private space in the northern sector of the shinden, then adjuncts to the north provided completely separate

53 **Kyoto, Imperial Palace.**

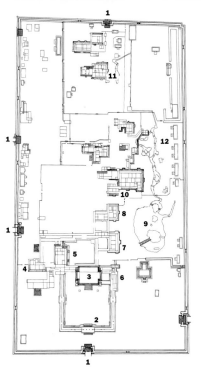

54 Kyoto, Imperial Palace plan.

(1) Outer gates; (2) Jomei-mon; (3) Shishin-den (Hall for Ceremonial Occasions); (4) Shodaibu-no-mar; (5) Seiryo-den (Hall for Lesser Ceremonial Occasions); (6) Giyo-den (antechamber); (7) Ko-gosho (Sleeping Hall of the Crown Prince); (8) Ogakumon-jo; (9) lake garden; (10) Tsune-goten (Sleeping Hall for Withdrawal to the Private Garden); (11) Kogo-goten; (12) private garden.

The original imperial palace (Daidairi) of Heiankyo was built in 794 for the emperor Kammu on the model of the one at Heijokyo (see 30, page 71) but further departed from symmetry in the placing of the imperial private quarters (Dairi) off-axis to the east. The complex as a whole was centred at the head of the great north–south axis that was to divide the new capital into halves, as at Heijokyo. But the western half of the urban project was never realised and the emperor moved further east to a detached palace (Sato-dairi) after disaster had struck the Daidairi. The eastern palace became the official imperial residence in 1331 but was damaged by fire many times. It was rebuilt in 1788, after the fire which destroyed much of Kyoto, and again in 1855 in reproduction of its original Heian form.

55 **Kyoto, Imperial Palace, Shishin-den.**

The grandest hypostyle hall of the complex, containing the imperial thrones (Takami-kura for the emperor, Micho-dai for the empress), this was used for the installation of emperors and other major court ceremonies. It is of unpainted wood and is partitioned only to form a retiring space at the back (north). The roof is thatched. Note the asymmetrical connection with the antechamber.

56 **Kyoto, Imperial Palace, Shishin-den** interior.

57 **Kyoto, Imperial Palace, Shodaibu-no-mar** eastern verandah and corridor.

In the Heian period the emperor lived in a shinden similar in profile but smaller than the Shishin-den, but moved to less formal quarters later, leaving the Shodaibu-no-mar for ceremonial occasions of less importance than those accommodated in the Shishin-den, where internal partitioning is much less extensive and flexible.

58 **Kyoto, Imperial Palace, Ko-gosho** from the north.
Another shinden, internally screened beyond an east-facing corridor, this was the residence of the crown prince. Furthering the process apparent in 13th-century works such as the Shoryoin (prince Shotoku's shrine terminating the dormitory) at Horyuji, the main gables are elaborated with barge boards and pendant finials to the purlin ends.

rooms, and finally the latter were detached in free-standing pavilions and the shinden was left free for ceremonial activities.

As Chinese influence receded with the decline of the Tang in the 10th century, strict formality was relaxed. Indeed, it was in their approach to the design and siting of their houses – where eternity was obviously not an important consideration – that the native predilection for the informal achieved its full expression. From the air (see 53, page 117), it is clear how the Imperial Palace at Kyoto reflects the various stages in the evolution of the Japanese tradition at its grandest: the Chinese formality – even the Chang'an prototype – is still marked, but the symmetry of the main court is disturbed to the right of the main ceremonial hall by the corner buildings leading to the residential quarters (see 54 [1], page 118). These are devolved back into the site informally (see 54 [2–4], page 118), on a diagonal, addressing a small, artificial lake on the way to the complete seclusion of the emperor's private garden.[59]

The garden

Beyond mastery of the asymmetrical, the most characteristic feature of Japanese architecture is the directness with which buildings relate to their environment, complementing nature. From the outset, the Japanese have sought to live in harmony with nature rather than in opposition to it; even in their primitive pit-dwellings the portico extending before the door broke down the barrier between internal and external space, integrating house and site (see 1, page 6). This was the origin of the verandah. With its development went landscaping.

The Japanese garden is a reproduction of natural scenery within restricted confines: mountains, streams, lakes or seas, and plants are reproduced in miniature – or at any rate to a scale suited to the scope of the site. Texts dating back to the 11th century, not least the *Sakuteiki* (*Account of Garden Making*), deal with the recreation of nature in the small space of a garden and even the self-conscious emulation of celebrated beauty spots. Doubtless drawn from earlier sources, there is a 15th-century treatise on deployment of the elements – rocks, water, plants – for the eliciting of atmosphere. Ideally there should be six attributes: art and age, expansiveness and seclusion, spaciousness and abundant water. Unlike the Chinese, the Japanese rarely partitioned even urban gardens

59 **Kyoto, Imperial Palace, private garden.**

into distinct rooms. Literature and excavation reveal, however, that from the earliest period of Sinification at Heijokyo, a pond or lake was central to the design, no doubt always with a circuit disclosing a variety of ideal views. The lady Murasaki Shikibu, who wrote *The Tale of Genji* early in the 11th century, knew such gardens. The focal lake, certainly, was a key element in the evocation of the western paradise at Hojoji and Uji (see 50, pages 110–111) and in the reconstructions of the Fujiwara and Imperial Palaces of Kyoto (see 52 and 54, pages 115 and 118) – but that takes us well beyond the Heian period.

To counter the forces of monasteries like Enryakuji and of feudal local clan chiefs, the resurgent emperors of the late Heian period formed a body of guards from two great clans of imperial descent, the Taira and the Minamoto, who had both been distinguished in fighting against the Ainu. Conflict over the imperial succession in 1156 was won by the Taira, but their corrupt and dictatorial rule led to further trouble from which the Minamoto emerged victorious in 1185. Wielding power through his camp office (*bakufu*) at Kamakura – near modern Tokyo, far from the seductions of the court – their leader Yoritomo established military government, in principle over his own people, in practice over the empire. The title *Shogun* (Barbarian-defeating Great General) was revived for him, and the emperor and the regent both remained in place. Yoritomo's successors proved decreasingly effective, however, and the Hojo family of one of their wives even established an equivalent to the Fujiwara regency at Kamakura. Duality was doubled.

The Kamakura period of military rule saw the introduction of Chan (Zen) Buddhism to complement the Jodo sect and other esoteric ways to salvation in the Heian period. Thus, as in China, there were multiple strands of Buddhism in Japan: to the ways to salvation through merit won personally with works or through faith in the agency of outside powers – especially the Amida Buddha of the Pure Land – was now added a wholly inner way. Rejecting dogma as inimical to ultimate truth, the Zen returned to the idea of personal enlightenment, to the essence of Buddhahood, characterised as the 'inner light of the Buddha heart' in every individual. Dormant, it needed awakening, and that was achieved through a special meditative yoga. Promoting discipline of mind and body, self-realisation and self-help, rather than relying on others or seeking escape from responsibility by shifting the burden onto others, Zen also recognised the idea of self as egotism that must be shed for salvation, and the warrior was particularly attracted to its peculiar form of asceticism. Indeed, the military regime favoured Zen with its patronage to the almost total disadvantage of the esoteric sects that had enjoyed the attentions of the rulers of Heiankyo and then overawed them.

In 1274 and 1281 the Mongol emperor of China, Kublai Khan, attempted to invade Japan. On both occasions he was driven back by exceptionally severe storms. The Storm god Susanowo and the Shinto gained the credit. The *bakufu* had lost it: the cost of mounting a defence had impoverished Yoritomo's regime and, unable to pay the troops, he was discredited. Opposition crystallised around an unusually forceful emperor, Go-Daigo. He was deposed, but he rallied his forces and overran Kamakura in 1335. However, one of his supporters – a Minamoto turncoat called Ashikaga Takauji – betrayed him, deposed him again and re-established the shogunate at Muromachi – a suburb of Kyoto – by 1338.

At first the Muromachi regime promoted a rival to Go-Daigo's legitimate successor as emperor, who had retreated from Kyoto to Yoshino in the south: thus there were two imperial courts until the third Ashikaga *shogun*, Yoshimitsu (1367–1408), suppressed Yoshino. Yoshimitsu was effective in general, but the power of his successors to overawe the *bakufu* proved limited, and from the mid-15th century Japan was constantly racked by violence. Yet trade prospered and contacts with China were strengthened. Before the end of the 1540s the Portuguese had introduced themselves from Macao off the Chinese coast. With them came the first Christian missionary, St Francis Xavier.

His Jesuit followers had remarkable success in their proselytising mission, especially in Kyushu.

Despite the conservatism common to religious builders everywhere, the Buddhists diversified form and style for the specific purposes of varied sects in the Kamakura period. Three main styles emerged: the 'Indian' (tenjikuyo), the 'Chinese of the Zen' (karayo) and the 'Japanese' (wayo) derived from the Heian legacy. Ultimately there was some cross-fertilisation, particularly between the 'Zen Chinese' and the 'Japanese' styles.

The 'Japanese' style of temple

The style originally imported from the mainland in the Heijokyo period and adapted by Heian builders during the ascendancy of Kyoto was called 'Japanese' under the Kamakura rulers to distinguish it from the newly imported mainland styles, somewhat misleadingly called 'Chinese' and 'Indian'. The development of the orthodox 'Japanese' style had been furthered by the Fujiwara to lend an aura of legitimacy to their favoured Pure Land sects, and the esoteric Shingon and Tendai sects followed suit to assert their claims to orthodoxy. Though essentially conservative,

60 **Nara, Kofukuji, south-eastern main image hall and pagoda.**

Burnt by Taira in 1180, Kofukuji was rebuilt over the next 30 years, but subsequent destruction left only the small western pagoda. The five-story eastern pagoda (at 55 metres/180 feet Japan's tallest) and main image hall were rebuilt c. 1415.

the 'Japanese' style was to admit of development, and even to be influenced by the newly imported continental styles. However, this was not yet apparent in the rebuilding of Nara's Kofukuji after 1180, or even in its subsequent rebuilding in the 15th century.[60] Survivals from the Kamakura period are rare: among

61 Ishiyamadera, single-storey pagoda late 12th century, built by Yoritomo Minamoto (1147–99, effective ruler after 1181).

A type of single-storey pagoda was developed from the Indian stupa by the esoteric sects in the Heian period to enshrine relics and secure treasure. There are no survivals, but images on *mandala*s, cosmic circular diagrams for meditation, show that initially, at least, the bulk of its mass was a cylinder and hemisphere – or at any rate a dome on a drum – over which a canopy was represented by a broad-eaved roof of the traditional Japanese kind. As the Japanese were unused to masonry, the dome was probably of plaster on a timber frame, and thus was perishable. Drum and dome were encased in trabeated cubicles, one over the other and each with a roof. The triumph of elegant trabeation over sturdy mass is clearly distinguishable in the perpetuation of late Heian aesthetic values.

62 **Nara, Yakushiji, Toindo** 1285.

In line with the Kamakura regime's desire to assert legitimacy, most of the restoration work carried out after the destructive rivalry between Taira and Minamoto was conservative, as here: indeed while the interior has the light elegance of the late Heian style, the exterior goes further back and recalls some late Heijokyo strength.

63 **Nara, Yakushiji, Toindo** interior.

pagodas, the single-storey version (tahoto) of Ishiya-madera is unique,[61] while the Toindo of the Yakushiji monastery at Nara is one of the most substantial temple halls in the 'Japanese' style.[62-63]

The esoteric sects rejected rigid axial symmetry in the disposition of the numerous halls of their complexes, having regard to the contours of usually remote mountain sites. Beyond the addition of an antechamber to provide extra space for worshippers in front of the images in the nave (see 48, page 106), the increasingly abstruse rites of these sects prompted the doubling of the sanctuary (naijin) with an area for worship (gejin), and, augmented by this extra space, the main hall (hondo) was clearly the dominant element in the complex. Given that the logic of the structural system was masked by ceilings of the type with a hidden roof frame (noyane), greater freedom of planning allowed the elimination of columns to clear space of obstruction.[64] On the other hand, the area for worship was screened from the sanctuary with lattice and this admitted disparity in the height of their ceilings – elevated over the great images, lowered to intensify the space of the worshippers.[65]

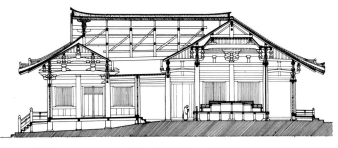

64 **Heijokyo (modern Nara), Todaiji, Hokkedo (Hall for Meditating on the Lotus Sutra)** lateral section.

The original main image hall of Konshoji (see 32, page 73) was augmented towards the end of the 12th century with a free-standing antechamber joined to it by a corridor (without destroying the integrity even of its roof).

Parallel pavilions were often linked in this way with a bridging arm. The more important examples include the 10th-century Kitano Shrine in Kyoto, rebuilt in the 17th century.

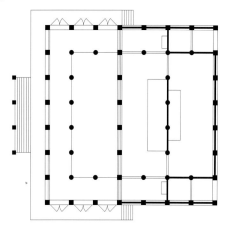

65 **Kora-machi, Saimyoji** 13th century, plan and lateral
section (right).

The typical 'Japanese'-style plan was rectangular and
partitioned laterally, at the second or third column of the
side ranges, into an open front section for worshippers and
an enclosed sanctuary that might be subdivided to form a
sacristy behind the image chamber. Where the main division

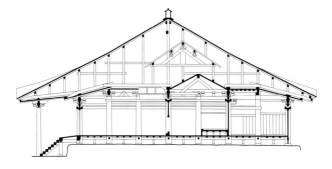

took place at the third column – or later – intermediate
supports were necessary in the worshipping area, preserving
the distinction between it and the antechamber. According
to the extent of the former, or the extension of the roof over
the porch, the section might depart from the symmetrical
norm. Brackets and struts follow late Heian precedents, but
the frog-leg struts are usually more elaborately decorative.

The 'Indian' style

Despite its name, the 'Indian' style was imported from southern China by the monk Chogen (1121–1206) specifically for the huge structure required to shelter the colossal statue of the Buddha in the rebuilding of the Todaiji complex at Nara after its wanton destruction by the Taira in 1180. The style is characterised by a vast double-height space with continuous pillars and no ceiling. Its rainbow-beams, pronounced in their curvature, are separated by bottle-shaped struts (taiheizuka) instead of the familiar cylinder or the frogleg form first imported from Wei China. Most distinctive, however, are its brackets stepped out through six tiers perpendicular to the building line, without lateral arms but braced with continuous tie beams parallel to the building line. The Todaiji Nandaimon (Great South Gate) survives as the only important representative of Chogen's original work.[66–67] His Daibutsuden (Great Buddha Hall) was destroyed in 1567 and ultimately was replaced by a lesser building in an 'Indian'-style permutation for the patched-up Buddha.

66 **Nara, Todaiji, Nandaimon** 1196–1203.

67 Nara, Todaiji, Nandaimon lateral section.

Restoration of Todaiji after it was commissioned by the former emperor Shirakawa (who reigned between 1155 and 1158, but retained effective power) was directed by the monk Chogen and paid for by the Minamoto leader Yoritomo (who had finally triumphed over the Taira). From this campaign, only the Nandaimon survived destruction by the forces of Matsunaga Hisahide in 1567. Of five by two bays (28.8 by 10.8 metres/95 by 35 feet and 25 metres/82 feet high) it set the standard for the monumental gate, and was emulated many times – though the proportions of the storeys were adjusted. With its vast double-height space rising to the apex of the roof without ceiling, between continuous posts bearing six-tiered brackets for the eaves of both storeys, it is the greatest surviving example of the 'Indian' style. The mode is exceptionally rare, but some of its characteristics were introduced to the renovation of Todaiji's Kaisando (Small Founder's Hall) in the mid-13th century.

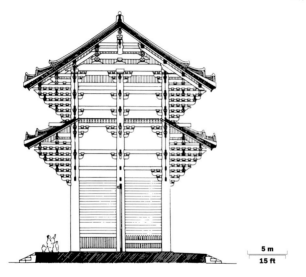

5 m
15 ft

The 'Zen Chinese' style

No more typically Chinese than the Tang forms of the preceding age, the 'Zen Chinese' style was imported from Sung Hangzhou by the monk Eisai (1141–1215) who introduced Zen Buddhism. Zen austerity and modesty of scale is the hall-mark of the style, in principle, but as the sect attracted patronage from the circle of increasingly opulent *shogun*s, elaboration of the inherited tradition was admitted to the main halls of the grander establishments – not least, the manipulation of the traditional structural frame to support broad ceilings over radically expansive naves without intrusive posts but with intermediate bracket-clusters (instead of struts) and multiple lever arms. Even in the modest context of the subtemple, where the Zen monk lived, austerity was moderated by the introduction of the elegant undulating 'Chinese' gable (karahafu) and cusped arched window (katomado).

Nothing survives from Eisai's period or from the rest of the 13th century, but the earliest 14th-century traces at Kenchoji, Kyoto, conform to the traditional axial plan. The main components – gate, image and lecture halls, but rarely pagodas – also follow Heian

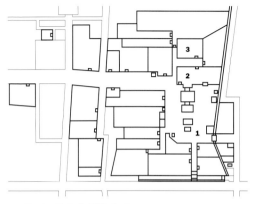

68 Kyoto, Daitokuji block plan.

(1) Main axis, sammon to the main shrine building and lecture hall; (2) Honbo (abbot's quarters); (3) Daisen-in subtemple. The blocks to the east and west of this central core have many other subtemples.

The complex occupies the site of the hermitage of the Zen master Shuho Myocho (1282–1337) who taught the emperor Hanazono (1308–18) and thus attracted imperial support. The complex reached its apogee in the 17th century.

precedent in their symmetry. Indeed, the gatehouse is characteristically of three bays of two storeys with side stairs known as sammon ('triple' or 'mountain' gate), while butsuden (main shrine building) and hatto (lecture hall) are grand structures with the full panoply of brackets, like the 'Japanese' style, wide central bays and flat ceilings to distinguish the nave from the surrounding ancillary space. Beyond and beside the main complex are various subtemples, including extensive quarters for the abbot (hojo), and these are generally asymmetrical in distribution around enclosed gardens.

The Kyoto Daitokuji may be taken as representative:[68] opened with the earliest surviving example of a sammon,[69] the main axis leads through the principal halls[70-72] to a complex of subtemples,[73-75] which is among the most extensive – and earliest – of its kind in Japan.

69 Kyoto, Daitokuji, Sammon 1526–89.

Equipped with a generous space for images on the upper floor, as in the Nandaimon at Todaiji (see 66–67, pages 143 and 145) but slightly reduced in height to avoid top-heaviness,

stairs were needed. They could not be incorporated in the
body of the building without inhibiting passage through it,
so they were erected to the sides – sometimes in detached
towers connected to the main structure by a bridge.

70 Kyoto, Daitokuji, Butsuden (1665) and Hatto (1636).

71 Kyoto, Daitokuji, Butsuden lateral section.

   The elimination of intermediate posts for the unimpeded expanse of the nave, under a flat ceiling, is typical of the grander aspects of the 'Zen Chinese' style – though consistent with Zen abstraction. To relieve residual stress on this scale, given the massive timbers needed for the span, intermediate brackets were incorporated over thickened beams between the columns. Paradoxically, the doubled

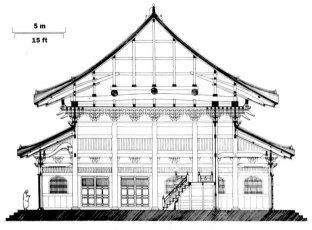

lever-arm ends are purely decorative (in this case), their
continuity and structural role interrupted by the huge
hidden beams from which the ceiling is suspended and
on which the roof frame rests. Multiplication of once-
structural elements for decorative purposes was
characteristic of Chinese architecture after the apogee
of the Song in the 12th century. Note the cusped arch of
the window.

72 **Kyoto, Daitokuji, Butsuden** interior.

73 **Kyoto, Daitokuji, Daisen-in** entrance court.
Built in 1513, the main building at the subtemple consists
of three rooms to the north doubled by three facing south
through a verandah to the enclosed gravel garden. The
incorporation of a 'Chinese' gable over the entrance gate
and the porch is characteristic of the 'Zen Chinese' style,

and was to have a great future in Japan. It appears –
precociously, perhaps – over the central shrine doors inside
the Shotoku chapel at the end of the dormitory wing of
Horyuji. The main gables show some departure from the
representation of the purely structural beam and strut, ridge
pole and purlin ends: pendants conceal the latter at least.

74 **Kyoto, Daitokuji, Daisen-in** shrine room.

The central chamber in the southern Daisen-in range is the shrine. Its simplicity and austerity are typical of the style in essential principle.

Daisen-in is celebrated for the screen paintings of the masters Soami (1472–1523), Kano Motonobu (1476–1559) and Kano Yukinobu (1513–75).

75 **Kyoto, Daitokuji, Daisen-in** shoin.

The northern range was for sleeping and for study, with the latter incorporating a shoin or 'book room'. 'Shoin' derives from the scholar's study with its asymmetrically disposed shelved alcove for books projecting to the exterior like a blind oriel.

The Zen garden and tea-making

Seeking enlightenment in total self-abnegation through intuition inspired by meditation on the meaning of the universe revealed in natural phenomena, seeking unity with nature, Zen promoted the laying-out of gardens. In contrast with the literal reproduction of nature, derived by the Heian masters from the Chinese, but in line with the general austerity of their way to salvation, Zen Buddhist gardeners preferred abstraction calculated to elicit a subjective response. Though some planting is admitted, rocks and raked gravel or moss alone usually represent the primary features of the natural world, earth and water. These dry landscapes are not entered (except for the cathartic activity of maintenance) but contemplated in meditation on the significance of natural phenomena. The Daisen-in of the Daitokuji has an important example (see 73, page 153), but the most celebrated dry gardens in Japan belong to another foundation of the Kamakura period, the Ryoanji subtemple of the Myoshinji.[76–77]

A related event of great significance for the design of gardens and residences was the development of tea-making into an abstruse ceremony of great subtlety, concentrating the mind on the elimination of

76 Kyoto, Ryoanji, gravel garden.

A villa with a pond garden inherited by Hosokawa Katsumoto c. 1450 was transformed in 1488 by his son, Masamoto, into a shrine to his memory as a subtemple of the Myoshinji. The abbot's quarters were rebuilt in 1681, but the main garden, in which 15 rocks in five informally related groups are surrounded by a sea of sand, is usually thought to be at least a generation earlier.

77 **Kyoto, Ryoanji, moss garden.**

inessentials. Tea had been introduced to Japan in the 8th century, but it had become a ritual particularly in the Zen context: at first the host was served with his guests in a room with a view. By the end of the 15th century, however, the intensity of concentration that the ritual sought to induce admitted no distracting view; indeed the garden was organised so that the path to the blind tea room symbolised a return from engaging artifice to the primitive purity of undefined wilderness.

Muromachi palaces

In the Kamakura period the essentially symmetrical shinden continued to dominate the imperial palace complex, though this might be asymmetrical in its general distribution. The *de facto* rulers and their entourage resorted to the radically asymmetrical shoin or 'book-room'. Alcoves were occasionally incorporated in the latest shinden to form the hybrid structure called a shuden. Scroll paintings are still the main sources of information for this period, but mature examples of the shoin type of palace buildings survive from after the Muromachi era.

The secular form originated from the diversification of elements within the palace compound: the shinden

78 **Garden pavilions** detail from a 15th-century scroll painting of the life of prince Shotoku (Kyoto National Museum) (see 27 and 51, pages 57 and 114).

The shinden survives, at top, as do the galleries linking it to less pretentious pavilions. Now, too, there are several small, open kaishos distributed informally in the garden, especially in relationship to the lake which still provides the nucleus of the scheme – as under the Fujiwara and, particularly, in *The Tale of Genji*.

was retained for ceremonial purposes, though more extensively partitioned than in the Heian period, but the informally related elements of the private quarters were detached and distributed in sympathy with the configuration of the garden as 'meeting places' (kaisho) for relaxed retreat.[78] This development was furthered, if not initiated, at the end of the 14th century in the palace built for the retirement of the *shogun* Ashikaga Yoshimitsu in an earlier pond garden in Kyoto. The only surviving element is the so-called Kinkaku (Golden Pavilion), a kaisho converted into a shrine dedicated to the patron (Kinkakuji).[79]

The principal Muromachi seat in Kyoto, rebuilt by Ashikaga Yoshinori (1394–1441) had a shinden and three kaishos. These are all lost, but conjectural restoration is based on near-square plans subdivided into northern and southern ranges of rooms, some with a projecting bay next to an outer corner. To supplement contemporary descriptions and scroll paintings, evidence for this is drawn from the surviving elements of the retirement villa built from 1482 for Yoshinori's son, Yoshimasa (1436–90), which was also later converted into a dynastic shrine (Ginkakuji): the Ginkaku (the so-called Silver Pavilion) and Togudo

79 Kyoto, Kinkakuji, pond garden with Kinkaku 1397, rebuilt 1955. The pond garden is c. 1220.

In 1397 the garden's proprietors (the Saionji family) were forced to cede it to Yoshimitsu, who built the extensive Kitayamadono palace thereafter. The three-storey elevation of the surviving pavilion derives from an ostensibly 'Chinese-style' dependency of the late 12th-century Amida temple of Saihoji (west of Kyoto, on the site of a palace of prince Shotoku), which Yoshimitsu avowedly emulated in the design of both his palace and its setting. The prototype was presumably a side pavilion joined to a shinden-style main hall by galleries, as in the palaces of the Fujiwara and their Tang models. Whether that was originally the case here too, the square plan subdivided into northern and southern ranges of rooms is typical of the kaisho as it developed in complete detachment.

80 **Kyoto, Ginkakuji, pond garden with Ginkaku** 1482.

Like Kinkakuji (see 79, page 162), much in the Ginkakuji
scheme derives ultimately from Saihoji, including the
garden. The Ginkaku enshrines Kwannon in a small chapel
among its reception rooms.

81 **Kyoto, Ginkakuji, pond garden with Togudo tea house** 1486.

tea house.[80-81] Supposedly covered in silver, the Ginkaku was inspired by the Kinkakuji, but it has only two storeys and the lower one is a development of the shoin. In the Togudo the shoin approaches maturity. An alcove for sitting in (tokoma) was incorporated into the design of the west front, alcoves for writing in (tsukeshoin), for storing documents in (chigaidana), and for displaying decorative objects in (tokonoma) distinguish the north-west corner room, which is thought to be the earliest-surviving tea room in Japan.

The Muromachi period was ended by Oda Nobunaga, a local clan chief of central Honshu who had reduced all his neighbours to submission by 1578. He eliminated the military might of monasteries like Enryakuji that had taken sides against him, and fortified his base at Azuchi with the first of the great castles from which power would henceforth be wielded. On his early death in 1582, his mission to re-unify Japan was taken up by his vassal Toyotomi Hideyoshi and his ally Tokugawa Ieyasu. Setting aside their initial rivalry, they cooperated to overcome the remaining opposition by 1590. This included the Christians – Spanish now, as well as Portuguese – whose aggressive methods seemed to aim as much at temporal as spiritual imperium. An edict of 1587 expelling all foreign priests, but not the merchants, contained the situation for a time, though it was not in fact fully implemented.

Dedicating his services to the emperor, Hideyoshi obtained the Fujiwara title of *Kampaku* – but recognised that only a Minamoto could be *shogun*. He built magnificently, most notably the Jurakudai palace on the site of the old imperial Daidairi in Kyoto, and Osaka castle as his main stronghold. He attempted to secure his position by directing the unruly local clan chiefs against Korea in 1592. The expedition was disastrous, but the protracted struggle ended only after his death in 1598. Tokugawa Ieyasu asserted himself to fill the void, dismissing a final challenge from his rivals at Sekigahara in 1600 and eliminating Hideyoshi's young heir in 1615. As a Minamoto, he claimed the shogunate and established it at Edo (now Tokyo, the 'Eastern Capital').

Hideyoshi had disarmed the populace, imposed a caste system based on profession, tied the peasants to the land and consolidated feudalism by designating lords of the manor to raise levies for the central authority. Ieyasu re-allocated the fiefs among three categories of clan chief – members of his clan, their allies at Sekigahara and the beaten opposition. Naturally the best land and the most important strategic positions went to the first of these who were allowed to fortify them with castles as the seats of provincial administration. All other castles had to be demolished, but the local clan chiefs were accorded considerable autonomy so long as they manifested loyalty to the *shogun*.

The foreigners also had to be dealt with. To the Portuguese and Spanish, the Dutch were added in 1605.

Their rival pretensions, political and doctrinal, served only to turn suspicion into xenophobia at a time of stress when a new regime was establishing itself. The expulsion of foreigners had been decreed several times since the edict of 1587, but in 1639 it was finally effected except for a small colony of Dutch traders on an island in Nagasaki bay. For nearly 250 years thereafter, order was enforced within and the outside world excluded. Naturally, for an enveloping centralism, that order was syncretic and eclectic, drawing on many strands of Japan's heritage.

The Tokugawa period

The Tokugawa period was peaceful, on the whole. With peace came prosperity for all except the imperial entourage at Kyoto, who subsisted in empty hereditary offices, and the redundant professional soldiers (*shizoku*, or pensioned *samurai*), retired in select quarters of castle towns where they turned either to learning or to decadence. By the 18th century the merchants had emerged predominant – economically. Socially inferior, these newly rich townsmen were beneath the contempt of the *samurai*, let alone the culture of the *shogun*'s court, and they lavished their resources on the gratification of sensuality. Many also invested in education. Inspired by inklings of western scientific achievement transmitted by the Dutch, their ranks were to foster opposition to the increasingly stultifying regime, destabilised in the 19th century by swollen bands of destitute ex-*samurai* (*ronin*).

Xenophobia, on the other hand, had encouraged introspection and a concern with the past – not least by the *samurai*. This, in turn, prompted a revival of interest in the indigenous religion and, through Shinto, the divine descent of the emperor sustained in Kyoto. All the greater, then, was the humiliation when the *shogun* was forced to grant a trade treaty to the Americans following the intrusion of a naval squadron under Commodore Perry in 1853–54. Other western powers followed with equally irresistible force: the 'Barbarian-defeating Great General' was not fulfilling his function. Resistance being futile, the pragmatic Japanese saw that it would be best to learn from the foreigners and to make a new start. After little more than a year the new *shogun* Keiki, appointed in 1866 on the death of his childless predecessor, surrendered his authority to the new emperor Meiji, who had succeeded his father early in 1867 at the age of 15.

Castles and their towns

An unprecedented campaign of fortification throughout provincial Japan produced more than 100 castles between the foundation of Azuchi by Oda Nobunaga in 1576 and the completion of the Tokugawa stronghold at Edo in 1639. By then many of them had been destroyed by the Tokugawa, in the cause of consolidating their hold on centralised power. Twelve important examples survive, however, illustrating the main phases of development in the great age of castle building, though the history of fortification in Japan is as old as internecine rivalry.

As elsewhere, the earliest forts in Japan consisted of little more than a sequence of wards surrounded by palisades of timber or rammed-earth on a precipitous crag, with a barracks compound below. A raised platform, guarding the entrance to the first ward, provided for the lookout. The introduction of the cannon after the advent of the Portuguese in the mid-16th century led to the abandonment of inaccessible sites and the development of the keep (tenshu) on a commanding eminence surrounded by stone ramparts from which the artillery could command the plane of approach.

By 1576, Nobunaga's castle at Azuchi consisted of a single, great tower keep, seven storeys high, based on a mound surrounded by moats and an extensive bailey within which the tortuous line of approach formerly provided by nature was reproduced by labyrinthine design. This was the model for later castles, as at Matsue.[82] Though cyclopean masonry had replaced timber for walls and podia by the time of Azuchi, timber remained the main structural material for the keep which, providing palatial accommodation, soared with the pretensions of the builder.[83] As the concrete manifestation of power, anticipated at Azuchi, these structures – formidable but out of reach of effective artillery – dominated the countryside for miles around. Nowhere is this better represented than

82 **Matsue, castle** 1607–11, from the south.

The castle was built by Horio Yoshiharu (1543–1611), who was made local clan chief of Izumo as the reward for his contribution to the Tokugawa victory at Sekigahara. Matsue was a fishing village on his advent, but Yoshiharu recognised the strategic significance of a natural port dominating the Sea of Japan coast of west-central Honshu, and prompted its rapid development as a military base and

centre of administration and trade. The five-storeyed keep is
still essentially a tower (30 metres/98 feet high) on a low
hill, dominating an ascending sequence of wards and
surrounded by a double moat (20 metres/66 feet high).
Renovated in 1642, it was spared serious damage in the
great ages of Japanese de-fortification (under the early
Tokugawa when Matsue was in the hands of their vassal
Matsudaira, and in the late 19th century under Meiji).

83 **Matsue, castle** timber structure, interior.

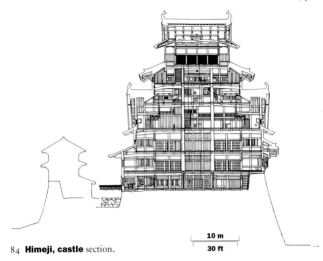

84 **Himeji, castle** section.

10 m

30 ft

85 PREVIOUS PAGES **Himeji, castle.**

Fortifying a strategic position south-west of Kyoto and west of Osaka, the main seat of Hideyoshi, the finest extant example of the Japanese castle was built by the Tokugawa supporter Ikeda Terumasa (1564–1613) immediately after the Tokugawa triumph at Sekigahara. The outer walls and barbicans, with their cyclopean bases rising from moats, are the most extensive in Japan (6 kilometres/3.6 miles in circuit). They embrace two low hills, Sagiyama to the west and Himeyama towards the centre. Only 50 metres (164 feet) high, but augmented by a massive podium rising through 30 metres (98 feet) in places, Himeyama hill supports the great keep (daitenshu) and a complex of towers linked by doubled walls around a roughly square court. In the time-honoured way of defence, the approach is punctuated by numerous gates that deflect it through a daunting elliptical course.

The seven storeys of the keep, built like the hulls of ships progressively diminished in size, are hung on a frame of massive timbers: one main post was originally dressed from a single trunk nearly 25 metres (82 feet) high. Mortice and tenon joints throughout provide enough flexibility for the structure to withstand earthquakes.

at Himeji, where variety was introduced by the asymmetrical diversification of mass.[84-85]

As the castles of the Tokugawa period provided for district administration, towns developed around their precincts. Most Japanese lived in the countryside, but towns had always grown up around the main seats of power and in the vicinity of important temples where the currents of pilgrimage, in particular, prompted the development of markets. In addition, station towns capable of servicing the grand entourages of great lords developed from staging-posts along the main roads, which formed the arteries of empire, and they too fostered markets.

In the later 16th century, when war lords moved from inaccessible crags to wield provincial power from eminences strategically placed on the junction of highways or by the estuaries of rivers, the castle town (jokamachi) eclipsed its predecessors.[86] Zoned in accordance with the profession and social standing of the inhabitants, the lord's entourage was at the top; artisans and traders, encouraged as sources of revenue, were in the centre and along the lines of communication respectively, while the pensioned *samurai* were in districts of their own.

86 **Toba, castle and town** model (Fisherman's Museum, Toba).

Built on a rocky promontory at the mouth of Nagoya bay, on the Pacific Ocean coast of central Honshu, a relatively primitive late 16th-century watch-tower keep was the nucleus for Toba's development with trade and the fishing industry in the 17th century. The organic growth pattern, governed by the topography, is typical of the castle town.

As part of the defence strategy, the streets continuing the exterior highways wind circuitously through the town, like the approach to the keep within the castle. Following the contours, and framing housing plots set back-to-back, this organic network sharply distinguishes most castle towns from the formally planned imperial capitals (see 29, page 64). As the economy developed in the Tokugawa period, markets were established in such towns, attracting merchants and, as always, the country came to town through the market, and the link is clearly discernible in housing.

Houses and gardens

Japan was predominantly a rural society until modern times, but few of the various types of farm house found in the regions of the archipelago before the 17th century have survived. It is assumed that the standard differentiation, still present thereafter, of a timber dais (toko) for sleeping raised from the earth floor (doma) of the entrance and general living area descends from the arrangement of the age-old pit-dwelling (see 1 and 2, pages 6 and 11). Like the temple pavilion, after Sinification the grander house was divided by its trabeated structure into a central area

87 **Yanohara farm house, Shirakawa district, Gifu Prefecture** c. 1750 (moved in 1960 to the Sankeien Garden Museum of Traditional Architecture, Yokohama), raised sleeping area.

Built entirely of wood bound with straw ropes and thatched, the house was of considerable opulence, fitting the social standing of its builder, Sasuke Iwase, as village headman (*shoya*) and one of the richest men in his district.

88 Yanohara farm house, Shirakawa district, Gifu Prefecture raised sleeping area, interior.

The ground floor (23 by 13 metres/75 by 43 feet) is divided between the typical multipurpose raised sleeping area and a range of rooms including the sophistication of the patron's private shoin. There are two levels of rooms for the family, and storage in the roof, though it is lit only through the gable ends.

(joya, corresponding to the nave) and ancillary
spaces (geya, corresponding to an aisle) surrounded
by open verandahs.[87-88] After the 17th century, at
least, areas for servants and storage were screened
from the rest of the raised sleeping area, largely in the
ancillary spaces, and the timber dais, which
expanded in the central area, was partitioned to provide for eating as well as sleeping areas in anticipation of the ultimate sophistication of its division into
rooms in the 19th century. Though diversified masses
and several storeys are common in some of the
peripheral regions, the central norm is a rectangular
pavilion with a steeply pitched thatched roof rising
directly from the outer posts of the verandah
or over a second storey revealed above the verandah
eaves (see 87, page 182).

Scrolls of the seventeenth century reproduce much
earlier pictures of town dwellings showing rows of
two-or-four-bay structures divided (like their country
counterparts) into a raised sleeping area and timber
dias.[89] Even at this basic level, though the house is
entered directly from the street, there is often a garden to the side. With the growth of towns at the
beginning of the 17th century, plots became longer

89 **Osaka, town housing and shops** scroll painting of the early Tokugawa period (Osaka Castle Municipal Museum).

and narrower, and houses higher. Though there were regional variants, as in the country the basic norm for burghers of modest means was a rectangular block with a file of three rooms in depth, opening into a continuous raised sleeping area to one side – possibly flanked by or terminating in a garden strip – and an elevation of two storeys. As affluence and social standing increased, so too did the size of the house and its garden.

Spaces were subdivided by sliding screen-walls, and extensions diversified the mass of the pavilions organically, even joining them to one another with a zig-zag corridor or an open gallery in place of the primitive raised sleeping area. In the main space, the only fixtures were shelves and cupboards in alcoves (shoin) – ostensibly fitting them for the reception of government officials. In part and in whole, the complex was ordered in accordance with the module of the tatami mats that covered the floor: their proportions governed the defined range of planning formulae derived from their number and disposition. The best examples survive in the *samurai* districts of castle towns like Matsue.[90–92]

90 **Matsue, Shiominawate district** a street of *samurai* houses.

91 **Matsue, Shiominawate district** *samurai* house,
entrance to the outer court and inner garden.

Essentially asymmetrical in distribution, according to the
configuration of roughly rectangular plots, the main block
of the house is usually to the side of the entrance court,
facing a garden on at least two sides. There is a free flow
of space from room to room in the open-plan interior

92 **Matsue, Shiominawate district** *samurai* house, the verandah from the garden.

(originally screened with laminated rice paper on slender timber frames, but here glazed) and out over a shallow verandah to the garden, which is enclosed and screened from the entrance court.

Palaces

The mature shoin (sukiya shoin), with alcoves of all
three kinds, was an essential element of grand houses
by the end of the 16th century.[93] Supplementing a
relatively formal shuden, for ceremonial reception, it
was particularly popular as a retreat for study and
especially the ritual that had developed around the
making and taking of tea both with war lords and the
abbots of Zen monasteries. In the mature shoin, too,
sliding screens of wood and paper were supplemented by panels with painted decoration screening
alcoves particularly for sleeping (chodaigamae). The
abbot's quarters of the Kyoto Daitokuji and Nishi
Honganji may be taken as representative. The latter
incorporates important elements moved from the
Kyoto palaces of Hideyoshi: the Karamon (Chinese
Gate, so-named because of its 'Chinese' gables) and
the Hiunkaku (Flying Cloud Pavilion),[94–95] if not the
sumptuous halls of the abbot's quarters. Built in
emulation of Hideyoshi's celebrated complexes, the
Ninomaru of the Tokugawa's Nijo castle is the greatest surviving secular example.[96–100]

Typical of the most opulent secular buildings and
monastic quarters built in the period of reconstruc-

93 **Sankei-en, Shin style (shoin construction), tea house** interior (now preserved in the Sankeien Garden Museum of Traditional Architecture, Yokahama).

94 Kyoto, Nishi Honganji, Karamon late 16th century,
view from inside the compound.

Announcing the sumptuously ornamented style with
which the Momoyama rulers and their Tokugawa
successors advertised their affluence, this lacquered and
gilded trabeated structure with its cruciform cypress-bark
roof reputedly came from Hideyoshi's palace of Fushimi on
the outskirts of Kyoto. This style of roofing with crossed
pitches, the one covering the entrance axis curved up into a
'Chinese' gable, the longitudinal one slightly concave in
profile, is characteristic of the main gates of palace
compounds.

95 Kyoto, Nishi Honganji, Hiunkaku.

Moved to its present site in the garden of the Honganji abbot's quarters c. 1610, this pavilion was Hideyoshi's retreat in the grounds of his Jurakudai palace in Kyoto, which was demolished after he had fallen out with his nephew to whom he had assigned it as his heir. Marking the apogee of the mature shoin, the three storeys of elegant withdrawing rooms are graded in scale and intimacy under varied roofs, the lower two distinguished with 'Chinese' gables. The square plan typical of the early kaisho has ceded to asymmetry in complete sympathy with the informal purpose and garden setting.

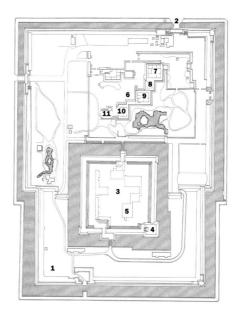

100 m

300 ft

96 **Kyoto, Nijo, castle** 1626, plan.

(1) Moated outer compound with (2) Higashi-Ote-mon
(Eastern Main Gate); (3) Honmaru with (4) keep (burnt
in 1750) and (5) palace pavilions (burnt in 1788);
(6) Ninomaru compound with (7) Tozamurai (Guard and
Antechamber Pavilion); (8) Shikidai (Reception Pavilion);
(9) Ohiroma (Ceremonial Audience Pavilion); (10) Kuro-
shoin (Private Audience Pavilion) and (11) Shiro-shoin
(withdrawing rooms).

The supreme example of the metropolitan castle on open
ground (hirajiro), with a defensive moat, cyclopean walls
and keep, the Kyoto residence of the Tokugawa *shogun*s
was begun by Ieyasu in 1569 and completed according to
the original plan by 1603: it then consisted of the moated
outer ward and moated inner Honmaru with its keep,
removed from Fushimi, and palatial buildings. In 1624,
Tokugawa Iemitsu added a second range of palace buildings
in the outer compound Ninomaru. Formidable as a work of
military engineering, the castle complex was designed
primarily to display wealth and power, eclipsing Hideyoshi's
Jurakudai palace.

The surviving Ninomaru suite has five halls: Tozamurai,
first in the sequence and largest (625 square metres/6700
square feet), is a square divisible by screens into some

tion after the civil wars of the 15th and 16th centuries – like the private quarters of the reconstructed Kyoto Imperial Palace, indeed (see 56 and 58, pages 121 and 123) – the Ninomaru at Nijo is a sequence of pavilions staggered along a diagonal axis linked by internal corridors that supplement – in part replace – the external verandahs of the old shinden type. Each block is divisible by retractable screens into compart-

10 compartments of widely disparate size for the *samurai* guard, waiting visitors and offices; the second and smallest, Shikidai, for the reception of dignitaries and their offerings by the *shogun's* ministers, is divided in the manner of the latest shinden into a south-facing hall and three north-facing chambers; third and grandest, the Ohiroma, is divided north–south into four main compartments: an armoury, an antechamber and a bipartite reception hall (Ichi-no-ma, or First and Second Grand Chambers) for visiting local clan chiefs who had not been Tokugawa allies at Sekigahara; the fourth, the Kuro-shoin, is divisible east–west into parallel chambers for the reception of Daiymo who had been allies at Sekigahara; and the fifth, the Shiro-shoin, small in scale and relatively modest in decoration, was for the ruler's use.

97 **Kyoto, Nijo, castle, Ninomaru, entrance and Tozamurai.**

98 **Kyoto, Nijo, castle, Ninomaru, Ohiroma** with the stepped arrangement of pavilions and the informal relationship with the garden.

99 **Kyoto, Nijo, castle, Ninomaru, Ohiroma** reception hall with the dais under a double-coved ceiling from which the *shogun* dominated his audience in the elongated single-coved auditorium.

100 **Kyoto, Nijo, castle, Ninomaru, Kuro-shoin** interior.

The pavilion is more intimate but no less opulent then the Ohiroma (see 99, page 199). Shoin alcoves, arranged for relief rather than for practicality, are inset with magnificent murals. Painted panels, usually with gold grounds, now screen each side and their opulence is extended into the frieze.

ments of varied size, the shuden and shoin prominent among them, proportioned in accordance with a limited number of standard arrangements of contiguous tatami mats, consistent in their dimensions. The trabeated structure, raised from the ground on posts, is surrounded by shallow verandahs and walled with non-load-bearing screens, often of a slender timber framework and paper, sometimes of timber slats or lattices. The monumental tiled roofs, gabled and hip-and-gabled, reveal intricately carved barge boards overlaid in gilt bronze.

Except for those of Hideyoshi, the chambers of the Tokugawa were unprecedented in their opulence. The shoin-style retreats of the court aristocracy, even of emperors, were less ostentatious. Inspired in particular by the mature tea house (sukiya shoin) of the pre-Tokugawa period, elegant if often capricious, they favoured an intimacy of scale, a simplicity of line and a restraint in monochrome ornament. Defined by bays standardised on the tatami module, they incorporated the essential range of shoin alcoves, but the alcove for sitting is usually deeper, with a tatami-covered floor of its own, and framed in a decorative moulding. The alcove for writing, too, is often assertively framed in

101 **Kyoto, Katsura Detached Palace** plan.

(1) Main gate; (2) Ko-shoin (Old Shoin); (3) Chu Shoin (Middle Shoin); (4) Shin Shoin (New Shoin); (5) Geppa-ro tea house; (6) Ama-no-hishidate ('celestial bridge'); (7) Shokin-tei (Pine Lute Pavilion); (8) Shoka-tei tea house; (9) Shoi-ken (Sense of Humour Pavilion).

Begun in 1616, the complex was enlarged over the next 40 years by the Hachijo line of imperial princes. There are three main buildings: the Ko-shoin built by prince Toshihito in 1616, the Chu Shoin built in 1641 by Toshihito's son, Toshitada, in preparation for his marriage, and the Shin Shoin built by the same prince in anticipation of a visit of his uncle, the retired emperor Mizunoo, in 1663. Toshihito also built the Geppa-ro and Shokin-tei tea houses. Toshitada rebuilt them and added two more, the Shoka-tei and Shoi-ken, between 1640 and 1655.

The Ko-shoin, Chu Shoin and Shin Shoin are staggered along a diagonal – like the main group of buildings in the Ninomaru at Nijo (see 96, page 194) – in the informal, additive manner, maximising views of the garden from the interior, and typical of the shoin. All have hip-and-gable roofs of shingle. Beyond verandahs, unbroken lines of sliding screens (shoji) can be entirely removed in summer for complete integration of exterior and interior.

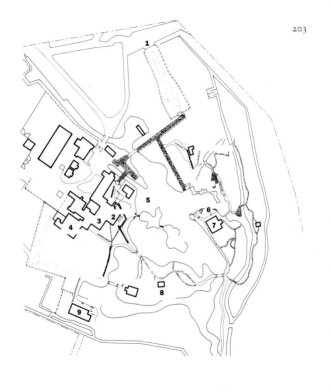

102 **Kyoto, Katsura Detached Palace** main complex.

103 **Kyoto, Katsura Detached Palace, Shokin-tei**
interior looking out over the garden.

The Shokin-tei is built in a self-consciously rustic style
(grass hut structure), with undressed timber posts,
rough plaster, an irregular massing and a part thatch,
part tile roof.

104 **Kyoto, Katsura Detached Palace, Shokin-tei**
interior.

The Shokin-tei has three rooms – one for tea, two for
withdrawing – and a kitchen. The first of the withdrawing
rooms is noted for its striking chequer-board patterned
screens and the view over the lake.

105 Kyoto, Katsura Detached Palace, Shoi-ken from the garden.

The largest garden pavilion at Katsura, the Shoi-ken has four compartments – one for the tea ceremony, two for withdrawing and a kitchen – like the Shokin-tei (see 103–104, pages 206–207).

106 **Kyoto, Katsura Detached Palace, Shoi-ken** interior.

From an inner room, there is a view out beyond the confines of the garden – a borrowed view, reminding the viewer of the real world beyond simulated paradise. It is a device recalling the principles of the Chinese gardener.

107 **Kyoto, Katsura Detached Palace** evocation of the Ama-no-hishidate in the garden.

On the Sea of Japan to the north-west of Kyoto, near Miyazu, a spit of sand covered in pines protects the lagoon of Aso. In poetry and mythological prose it is often

an ogee arch. The supreme example is the early 17th-century Katsura Detached Palace on the outskirts of the old imperial capital.[101-107]

The garden

The Japanese garden reproduces nature, real or ideal, in miniature or to full scale. Evoked in literature from at least as early as the era of the Fujiwara, when *The Tale of Genji* was written, it also responded to literature and constantly reproduced the images found there. At Katsura or the celebrated Kenrokuen of Kanazawa,[108] as in 7th-century Heijokyo, 11th-century Heiankyo and the lady Murasaki's imagery in *The Tale*, a lake is central to the design. The circuit around the lake in 'the stroll garden of many pleasures' (kaiyu) discloses a variety of real or ideal places – the aspects of one particularly venerable beauty spot, the Ama-no-hishidate, are

assimilated to the 'celestial bridge' from which Izanagi and Izanami, the productive deities in the mythology of the creation of the Japanese, created the islands of the archipelago. As such, it was designated as one of the empire's three main beauty spots.

108 **Kanazawa, Kenrokuen** 1676, river and glade.

Established in the outer ward of the castle, in the peaceful Tokugawa era, the garden is considered one of the most perfect in Japan for its evocation of the physical features of the natural world – river, glade, lake, sea, hill. The combination of the six attributes of a perfect garden – art and age, expansiveness and seclusion, space and abundant water – is enshrined in the name Kenrokuen.

evoked Katsura (see 107, page 210). And at Katsura tea houses may promote undistracted meditation but they prefer unbounded wonder at the beauty of nature (see 105–106, pages 208–209).

Temples and shrines

Not without Muromachi precedent, Momoyama and Tokugawa builders developed a hybrid style (setchuyo) from the cross-fertilisation of the 'Japanese', 'Zen Chinese' and even the 'Indian' styles in their vast programmes of reconstruction after the 300 years of internecine strife and destruction that followed the decline of the Kamekura *bakufu*. Apart from the Todaiji Daibutsuden, destroyed in 1567 but replaced with prolix eclecticism after 1684,[109–110] among the most prominent examples are the gates and halls of the Kyoto Choin and Nishi Honganji.[111–113]

Quite the most spectacular results of cross-fertilisation – bizarre some would say – are in the Tokugawa *gongen zukuri* ('incarnation structure') mausolea (reibyo) at Nikko on the slopes of the holy Mount Nantai. Nikko was not only colonised by the esoteric Tendai but also was dedicated to a rare syncretism between Shinto, Jodo and Zen in the abode of three fertility spirits identified as manifestations (*gongen*) of Amida Kwannon and Yakushi. Such a syncretism was clearly not without its appeal to the first Tokugawa, bent on reunifying Japan after centuries of internecine strife. He reputedly confided his wish to be buried on the mountain to the abbot of the Tendai Manganji, the principal temple of Nikko. The abbot removed his remains from Kuno-san, where they had been interred provisionally on his death in 1616. His mausoleum,

109 Nara, Todaiji, Daibutsuden.

Rebuilt to the specifications of the monk Chogen after its destruction by the Taira in 1180 but destroyed again by the forces of Matsunaga Hisahide in 1567, the Daibutsuden was repaired immediately and finally rebuilt between 1684 and 1709. It has seven by seven bays rather than the original eleven by seven, but it retains the double-height space, hipped roof and walled ambulatory under its own, lower, roof. The basic concept and elements such as the coffered ceiling are in the 'Japanese' style – indeed Heijokyan – but 'Indian'-style elements introduced by Chogen, particularly the brackets and braces (see 66–67, pages 143 and 145), were retained, and the undulating gable over the entrance is a 'Zen Chinese' feature.

110 **Nara, Todaiji, Daibutsuden** interior, with a patchy
reconstruction of the colossal image of Roshana.

111 **Kyoto, Choin, Sammon** 1619.

One of the largest temples in Kyoto, Choin was founded to protect the mausoleum of the priest Honen Shonin (1133–1212), one of the principal authors of the Shin Jodo sect. Largely destroyed in the civil strife of the 15th and 16th centuries, it was rebuilt under the patronage of the early Tokugawa *shogun*s. The Sammon emulates the Nandaimon of Todaiji in scale (see 66–67, pages 143 and 145) but amplifying the form of the Daitokuji Sammon (see 69, page 149) and is considered the masterpiece of the type.

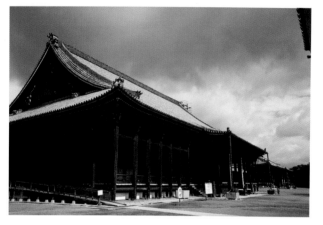

112 **Kyoto, Nishi Honganji, Goei-do (Founder's Hall)**
1636, with Hondo (Amidado, 1760) (background).

Founded in 1224 by the priest Shinran Shonin of the Shin Jodo sect, Nishi Honganji became the headquarters of the sect in 1591 with the blessing of Hideyoshi. The Goei-do (57 metres/187 feet long) marks the apotheosis of the gejin as a vast space for assembled worshippers before the

113 **Kyoto, Nishi Honganji, Goei-do** interior.

screened shrine to the founder and several other
compartments. To the north, but also facing east, the
Amidado (in which Amida is enshrined with prince
Shotoku) is only slightly less expansive.

114 PREVIOUS PAGES **Nikko, Toshogu, sanctuary.**

The Toshogu is unprecedented for its opulence, except by the palaces of Hideyoshi and the Tokugawa. At the top of a flight of steps, well within the sanctuary enclosure and beyond a range of storehouses, is the Yomei-mon (Gate of Sunlight). Within, the upper precinct is flanked by shrines including the Goma-do (Sacred Fire Temple) to the right and Mikoshi gura for reliquary palanquins to the left. In the centre, another elaborate Karamon, with 'Chinese' gables to all sides like the Yomei-mon but of only one storey, leads through a protective grille to the main sanctuary largely occupied by the tripartite Hon-den in which Ieyasu is venerated with Hideyoshi and Yoritomo. Gilding over-whelms the black lacquer of the basic trabeated structure.

Precedents for the type of tripartite complex with two buildings joined by a narrower gallery were found in the Kitano shrine in Kyoto, for example, built in the 10th century for Sugawara no Michizane and rebuilt under the second Tokugawa in 1607, and in the late 16th-century Hokoku shrine of Toyotomi Hideyoshi, also in Kyoto but destroyed. As to detail, once-structural elements were multiplied, contrary to structural logic (but in the case of the lever arm, not without precedent in Karyo practice), and transformed with ornament in disguise of practical purpose

115 Nikko, Toshogu, Yomei-mon.

As the ceremonial entrance restricting access to the Edo
élite, the Yomei-mon is a prodigiously ornamented, two-
storey variation on the type of the Karamon moved to the
Nishi Honganji from Hideyoshi's Fushimi.

(like the frog-leg strut that had begun as intermediate
support spreading the load of beams between columns, but
was now an excuse for sculptural ingenuity).

116 **Nikko, Daiyuin, shrine of Iemitsu** 1653.

In general, the second great Tokugawa shrine at Nikko, similar in style and derivation, is more restrained in sculptural detail, but the difference is purely relative in the case of the main shrine chamber, less hectic perhaps due to the more consistent use of gold on black.

117 **Nikko, Daiyuin, shrine of Iemitsu** portico.

118 **Tokyo, Meiji Jingu** 1920, reconstructed after war damage in 1958.

The Meiji Jingu enshrines the fertility spirits of the Meiji emperor (1868–1912) and his empress. A variant on the Nagare style of Shinto shrine, itself developed from the Shinmei style of Ise and, beyond that, the Yayoi granary, the Meiji Jingu amplifies the scale of the prototype to that of the

the Toshogu,[114-115] was not begun until 1634 under the direction of his grandson, Iemitsu, who built another for himself, the Daiyuin,[116-117] some 20 years later. These combine Shinto and Buddhist elements and transform them with the most elaborate ornament found on any Japanese building.

While constructing his grandfather's tomb, Iemitsu did much to consolidate the centralising structure of his state, and doubtless recalling the power of Tendai Enryakuji to overawe past administrations in Kyoto from its stronghold on Mount Hiei, he extended his patronage to the other sects at Nikko. Within little more than a decade the triad of fertility spirits had been enshrined in the huge Sambutsu-do, the largest building on the site, eclipsing the Manganji, which was rebuilt on a smaller scale as Rinnoji.

average Buddhist hypostyle main image hall. In place of the extended roof of the Nagare type, forming a portico, it incorporates the 'Chinese' gable which, crossed with the massive pitched roof, was common in Buddhist architecture – and shoin-style residences – since the great age of reconstruction began with the termination of civil strife by the Tokugawa in 1600.

119 **Tokyo, Meiji Jingu** entrance.

Conclusions

With the restoration of power to the Meiji emperor following the humiliation of the Tokugawa *shogun* by the Americans, foreign technology and foreign political ideals were readily espoused and Japan was transformed incredibly quickly. Still the emperor survived: patron of change, indeed, he emerged enhanced from the centuries of his eclipse. Traditionally he is believed to be of divine descent – but so too is his nation. With the reconstitution of the empire along western lines under the Meiji, the descent of the imperial line from Amaterasu was given new stress, distinguishing it from other Japanese, in line with European ideas of divine right. But if the emperor's descent was superior to that of his people, their descent from the divine entourage made them superior to all others. The consequences go far beyond the concern of this book – as do the details of Japan's transition from feudal obscurity to world power in little more than a generation. However, the revival of Shintoism and the proliferation of Shinto architecture along the lines preserved at Ise, also incorporating the imported hypostyle hall as it had developed over the millennium between Ise and Nikko, take our history of Japanese architecture full circle.[118-119]

glossary

AISLE side passage of a temple, running parallel to the nave and separated from it by COLUMNS or PIERS.

AMATERASU Sun Goddess. (See page 7.)

AMBULATORY semicircular or polygonal arcade or walkway.

ARCADE series of arches supported by COLUMNS, sometimes paired, and covered to form a walkway.

ATTIC, BLIND windowless roof-space.

BAKUFU military office. (See page 129.)

BALUSTER short COLUMN or PILLAR, usually bulbous towards the base, supporting a rail.

BALUSTRADE a row of BALUSTERS supporting a rail.

BARBICAN fortified structure at the entry to a town or city, often straddling a gateway.

BARGE BOARD board – usually decorated – at the gable end of the pitches of a roof.

BAY one of a series of compartments of the interior of a building, the divisions being created by PIERS or COLUMNS, for example.

BEAM horizontal element in, for instance, a TRABEATED structure.

BELFRY bell tower or the particular room in a bell tower where the bells are hung.

BILLET weight or block, usually of timber.

BODHISATTVA previous incarnation of the Buddha, a compassionate spirit.

BRACKET projecting structural element providing support.

CANOPY roof for a niche or statue, often supported by slender poles.

CAPITAL top part of a COLUMN, wider than the body of the SHAFT, usually formed and decorated more or less elaborately.

CHAMFER surface cut length-wise across the corner of a BEAM or POST.

CHIGAIDANA alcove for storing documents, in a mature SHOIN. (See page 166.)

CHIGI crossed FINIALS or ornamental additions to the roof of a SHINTO temple.

CHODAIGAMAE alcove for sleeping, in a mature SHOIN. (See page 190.)

CHODOIN administration precinct in imperial palace.

CHODO SEIDEN state reception hall in imperial palace.

CHOSHUDEN assembly hall in imperial palace.

CHUMON principal gate inside outer gate of a temple precinct.

CLERESTORY windowed upper level, providing light for a double-storey interior.

CLOISTER covered ARCADE, often around the perimeter of an open courtyard.

COFFERING decoration of a ceiling or VAULT with sunken rectangular or other polygonal panels.

COLONNADE line of regularly spaced COLUMNS.

COLUMN vertical member, usually circular in cross-section, functionally structural or ornamental or both, comprising a base, SHAFT and CAPITAL.

COVING concave moulding traversing the junction of wall and ceiling.

CUSP projection formed between two arcs, especially in stone tracery, hence CUSPED.

CYCLOPEAN MASONRY masonry made up of massive irregular blocks of undressed stone.

CYMA REVERSA wave-shaped moulding, the upper part concave and the lower convex.

DAIBUTSUDEN hall housing a massive statue of the Buddha.

DAIDARI imperial palace compound.

DAIGOKUDEN principal imperial hall of state.

DAIMYO provincial clan chiefs.

DAIRI private apartments in imperial palace.

DAIS raised platform, usually at one end of an internal space.

DAITENSHU great castle keep.

DOMA beaten earth floor of a farmhouse.

EAVES part of a roof that overhangs the outer face of a wall.

ENTASIS slight bulge in a COLUMN, designed to overcome the optical illusion of a straight column being slightly concave.

FINIAL ornament at the top of a GABLE or roof.

FRESCO painting done on wet plaster.

FUJIWARA family from which the KAMPAKU were drawn.

GABLE more or less triangular vertical area defined by the ends of the inclined planes of a PITCHED ROOF.

GEJIN area for worship in front of the main hall of a Buddhist temple complex.

GEYA space surrounding the central area of a house.

GIYO-DEN antechamber in imperial palace.

GONGEN ZUKURI type of hall embracing a sanctuary or incarnation structure. (See page 213.)

HINAYANA the lesser vehicle towards salvation in the Buddhist tradition (as opposed to MAHAYANA).

HINOKI cypress wood.

HIP angle formed at the meeting of two inclined planes on a hipped roof.

HIPPED ROOF *see* ROOF, HIPPED.

HIRAJIRO open ground on which castle is sited.

HISASHI roofed verandah in temple or dwelling.

HOJO apartment of the abbott in a 'Zen Chinese' monastery.

HONDO main hall of a temple complex.

HOZO treasure store in an imperial temple complex.

HYPOSTYLE HALL hall with a roof supported by many COLUMNS more or less evenly spaced across its area.

INTERCOLUMNIATION distance between two neighbouring COLUMNS, usually expressed in column diameters.

IZANAGI and IZANAMI, twin deities who gave birth to the Japanese islands. (See page 5.)

JOKAMACHI fortified castle town. (See page 179.)

JOYA central area of a house.

KAERUNATA see STRUT, FROG-LEG.

KAIDAN ordination hall or raised platform for the performance of the ordination ceremony.

KAIRO cloistered gallery in a temple.

KAISHO informal PAVILION set in a palace garden.

KAIYU traditional garden embodying symbolic aspects of nature.

KAMPAKU dynastic chief advisers to the emperors. (See page 88.)

KARAHAFU undulating 'Chinese' GABLE.

KARAYO 'Zen Chinese' style of temple architecture. (See page 132.)

KATOMADO cusped arched window.

KINGPOST principal vertical structural element supporting a roof.

KODO lecture hall in a temple complex.

KOFUN burial mound: by extension name given to a dynasty c. 300–700. (See page 13.)

KONDO central sanctuary building or image hall of a Buddhist temple.

KORYO curved lateral 'rainbow' BEAMS. (See page 42.)

KYOZO monastery library or SUTRA store.

LINTEL horizontal member over a window or doorway or bridging the gap between two COLUMNS or PIERS.

MAGOBISASHI verandah under the main roof of a building, often enclosing the HISASHI.

MAHAYANA the great vehicle towards salvation in the Buddhist tradition (as opposed to HINAYANA).

MANDALA cosmic diagram used in meditation.

MAUSOLEUM tomb, usually of a dignitary, built on a grand scale.

MEZZANINE intermediate storey, often between ground and first floors.

MICHO-DAI empress' throne.

MIKOSHI verandah with its own roof abutting main building.

MOKOSHI see MEZZANINE.

MORTICE AND TENON type of structural joint in which a slot in one element (mortice) receives a projection (tenon) from another.

MOSAIC decoration formed by embedding small coloured tiles or pieces of glass (tesserae) in cement.

MOYA central interior space of a building.

NAIJIN Buddhist temple sanctuary.

NANDAIMON south gate of a Buddhist temple enclosure.

NAVE central body of principal interior of a temple.

NICHE recess in a wall, often containing a statue.

NIO Buddhist guardian spirits.

NOYANE hidden roof. (See page 100.)

OGEE ARCH composed of two CYMA REVERSA mouldings meeting head to head at the apex.

OHIROMA ceremonial audience pavilion.

ORIEL projecting or bay window on an upper storey.

PAGODA Buddhist temple in the shape of a tower, usually with progressively smaller storeys, each with an elaborate ornamental projecting roof.

PALANQUIN covered litter with poles for carrying on the shoulders of bearers.

PALISADE defensive structure of wooden stakes driven into the ground.

PARAPET low wall, usually for defensive purposes.

PAVILION lightly constructed building, often tent-like and set in a garden.

PEDIMENT triangular area of wall, usually a gable.

PIER supporting PILLAR for wall or roof, often of rectangular cross-section.

PILE a POST or COLUMN set into the ground with others to provide foundation for a building.

PILLAR vertical element – structural or ornamental or both.

PITCHED ROOF *see* ROOF, PITCHED.

PODIUM projecting base or platform on which a building sits.

PORTAL doorway, usually on a grand scale.

PORTICO entrance to a building, generally featuring a COLONNADE.

POST vertical element in, for instance, a TRABEATED structure.

PRADAKSHINA AMBULATORY in Buddhist monastery.

PURLIN horizontal beam running the length of a roof, resting on the main RAFTERS and supporting the subsidiary rafters.

RAFTER roof timber, usually sloping down from the ridge to the EAVES, and supporting the outer covering of the roof.

RAINBOW BEAM *see* KORYO.

RELIEF carving, typically of figures, raised from a flat background by cutting away more (HIGH RELIEF) or less (LOW RELIEF) of the material from which they are carved.

RONIN warriors without any particular allegiance. (See page 170.)

ROOF, HIPPED roof composed of pitches with inclined (as opposed to vertical) planes at the ends.

ROOF, PITCHED roof composed of two inclined planes whose point of contact forms the ridge, and having vertical GABLES.

SACRISTY room in a temple for storing valuable ritual objects.

SAI-IN main compound of Buddhist temple.

SAKYAMUNI Prince Siddhartha, the Buddha. (See pages 36 and 67.)

SAMMON main gateway of Buddhist temple enclosure in the 'Zen Chinese' tradition.

SAMURAI hereditary professional warrior.

SARCOPHAGUS stone outer coffin, often highly decorated.

SESSHO hereditary regent. (See page 88.)

SETCHUYO hybrid style of architecture. (See page 213.)

SHAFT more or less cylindrical element of a COLUMN rising from the base to the CAPITAL.

SHAKA Japanese name for SAKYAMUNI.

SHINDEN principal building of a palace compound, generally in the form of a HYPOSTYLE HALL.

SHINGLES thin pieces of wood overlapping in the manner of tiles, to form a roof covering.

SHINNO MIHAIRA central post supporting a shrine. (See page 22.)

SHINTO native Japanese polytheistic religion. (See page 17.)

SHISHIN-DEN imperial audience hall. (See page 19.)

SHIZOKU pensioned SAMURAI.

SHODEN shrine building whose style is based on that of a granary. (See page 22.)

SHOGUN military leader or dictator. (See page 129.)

SHOIN originally library or alcove for reading: hence shoin style of building. (See pages 159 and 190.)

SHOJI sliding door composed of a wooden latticed frame covered with translucent white paper.

SHUDEN main reception room of a palace.

SHURO bell-tower of a Buddhist temple compound.

SOBO dormitory in a Buddhist monastery.

STRUT timber element, especially supporting a RAFTER.

STRUT, FROG-LEG strut in the shape of an inverted V. (See page 42.)

STUPA pre-eminent type of Buddhist monument, a tumulus, burial or reliquary mound.

SUKIYA SHOIN mature SHOIN or pavilion embracing space for tea ceremony among other things. (See pages 190 and 201.)

SUSANOWO Storm God.

SUTRA sacred Buddhist text.

TAHOTO single-storey PAGODA (See page 134.).

TAIHEIZUKA bottle-shaped STRUT.

TAISHA type of SHINTO shrine.

TAKAMI-KURA emperor's throne.

TATAMI rectangular floor-mats, of more or less standard size, made mainly of rushes.

TENJIKUYO 'Indian' style of temple architecture. (See page 132.)

TENON see MORTICE AND TENON.

TENSHU castle keep. (See page 171.)

TERRACOTTA baked clay used for construction or decoration of buildings or statues.

TESSELLATED describing a patterned surface composed of small blocks, such as MOSAIC.

TIE-BEAM horizontal member that supports and takes the thrust from two opposing RAFTERS.

TO square wooden tower serving as a reliquary. (See page 39.)

TOKO sleeping platform in a traditional farmhouse. (See page 181.)

TOKOMA alcove for sitting, in a mature SHOIN. (See page 166.)

TOKONOMA alcove for the display of decorative objects or paintings, in a mature SHOIN. (See page 166.)

TORII gateway to a SHINTO shrine. (See page 22.)

TRABEATED structurally dependent on rectilinear POST and BEAM supports.

TSUKESHOEN alcove for writing, in a mature SHOIN. (See page 166.)

TUMULUS ancient burial mound.

VAULT structure forming an arched roof over a space.

VERANDAH roofed COLONNADE attached to one or more sides of a building.

VESTIBULE courtyard in front of the entrance to a house; hallway to a building; space adjunct to a larger room.

VILLA country house.

WATTLE AND DAUB method of making walls using thin twigs (wattles) interwoven and then plastered with mud or clay (daub).

WAYO 'Japanese' style of temple architecture. (See page 132.)

The books listed below are those the author found particularly useful as sources of information on the architecture covered in this volume.

Masuda, Tomoya, *Japan*, Lausanne (no date)
Paine, Robert Treat and Alexander Soper, *The Art and Architecture of Japan*, New Haven and London 1981

bibliography

index

This is 25-volume series tells the story of architecture from the earliest settlements to the sophisticated buildings of the late twentieth century.